For Jasbir,

with every good creative
wish

SELECTED POEMS

Peter Abbs
Feb 13th — 02.

Previously published poetry by Peter Abbs

For Man and Islands (1978)
Songs of a New Taliesin (1981)
Icons of Time (1991)
Personae (1996)
Angelic Imagination (1997)
Love After Sappho (1999)

SELECTED POEMS

Peter Abbs

halfacro**w**n

h a l f a c r o w n

First published in Great Britain in 2002
by halfacrown publishers
198 Victoria Avenue
Kingston upon Hull HU5 3DY

Printed in Great Britain by
LSL Press, Bedford

ISBN 0 9542135 0 5

Cover image: *Hot June (*1995) © Harold Mockford
Reproduced courtesy of the artist.

FOREWORD

As our civilisation becomes ever more complex and materialistic it is in constant danger of disintegrating into functional parts and losing touch with the spirit of life. And this is where the poet and the power of poetry is most needed. For poetry at its most characteristic utters the passionate language of untiy. It aspires to wholeness of being. It discloses in the power of its metaphors and cadences the most unexpected connections and lines of development.

I believe poetry can illuminate bewildering complexity by locating its hidden centre and by expressing a profound symbolic language for its integration. In this I have always seen the function of poetry as essentially mythic and, however disturbing the content, on the side of healing.

It is impossible for me to know how far these poems speak the language of wholeness. I can only say that has been my intention and that it is for my readers and listeners to make the necessary judgements. Most of the poems gathered here have been written over two decades. They have been selected from six volumes, the first being published in 1978, the last in 1999. I have discarded all poems that seemed to me to fail for whatever reason and I have kept any revisions to a minimum, wanting each poem to speak with the voice it was originally written in.

To bring the *Selected Poems* into the new millennium I have also decided to include a number of new poems that have not been previously published. As always the aim is to look back in order to step forwards. I hope the new poems express further developments in my work so that, finally, this volume is not only retrospective but also prospective, not comfortably settling down but, rather, keeping faith with the ineffable spirit of life itself.

Peter Abbs
December 2001

for D

CONTENTS

from

FOR MAN AND ISLANDS

1978

IT

It skulks in the mind's undergrowth

In the dark thickets
It quivers close to the bed of rivers
A snake through the conflagration of grass
It is acquainted with stones and roots
Has wound itself many times round
The dripping tentacles of nature

At dusk it flies through the warp and weft of shadows
Compounds the darkness
Till large familiar things loom forward
Bulked with strangeness
Blackness humped upon blackness
Through which it lilts and slips

Where do I stand but where it was
And is no longer though
Something of its essence always lingers
Hangs fraily in the morning
From the bent bough's sodden foliage
Pervades a corner of the garden
A turning of the road

Disquieted I poke the ground
Dank arching grass blank stones
A thistlehead unloads its seeds
A bird flits through the charcoal thickets
The silence drums
I tread near the edge of some archaic memory
I can never reach
And spill a brief life writing
To allay the ache of it

A GIFT

Eithin ni bu fad. Taliesin. The Gorse was never prized.

Dawn smokes. I see
Gorse crackle over the slate's
Face. It swarms like bees. Is more
Imperious than
Torc or bronzed disc
Burnished. An emblem of transcendence. Each
Flower has
Power to heal the gashed memory
And put out to sea
The prudent heart.

Ishtar -
Astarte -
Aphrodite -
Magdalene -

I bring to you what things I can,
Things despised,
Unprized, spiked, feral.
This morning I bring
From the rock's throat, cynghanedd
Of barbed beauty.

Strange goddesses, do not turn your calm heads,
Nor let me disturb your coma -
I would not have your
Immortal litanies
Overheard
And put on record -

Now silence alone protects us.

FRAGMENT OF AUTOBIOGRAPHY

The earth was littered with signs we did not read or
Comprehend. In pits, where yawning holes swallowed rabbits,
We picked glossy blackberries or collected from the ground
Cold metal shapes, long, tapered, with frilled edges,
Chock-full with grit and sand. Harder than shale,
Whatever force had forged them, they were made to last.
Blankly we accepted them, bits from dislodged turf,
Fragments of the sliding screes we tried to scale.

On the Golf Links, coils of barbed wire poked through
Bramble bushes or uncurled themselves through bracken
And dangled from the cliff's ledges. We dived into
A labyrinth of tunnels, cluttered with fallen bricks
And junk, foul with urine. I did not mind
Nor did I heed the images in discarded papers, pages
Where ships sank, cities smouldered, planes trailed
Through the night. I saw only what our guileless games
Allowed, assumed the shelter's womb led out into the light.

In the Oak Woods we climbed the look-out tower,
Its mildewed wood sagged beneath our feet, we leapt
The missing steps. From the broken top, above the swirling trees,
We watched the summer fields, rippling with corn,
Streaked with scarlet poppies, end abruptly with the shore.
It was low tide, stranded on the white chalk beds,
A mine stared back at us with one blank eye.
But we stood up high, salt wind in our hair,
Cloud wisps in our hands, safe on the rotting planks.

THE DEATH OF THREE COCKS

He came punctually, at eleven, the hour he said.
I took him to the shed.
He upturned the first bird
And slipped the knife into its neck -

More crimson than its crown
The blood dripped to the ground -
Shocking in its redness -
And with one hand he kept the rent

Neck down. Mildly, he said
'I have seen this since I was a child
Following the heels of the butcher
Round the farms.'

With a kind of inward dread I took
The dead bird from his hands.
There was such commotion in its legs
And pinions, it appalled to hold it.

Obedient to the last transmission
Of the will, its mottled wings
Still fluttered, shut and shuddered-
Would not stay still.

Yet I must stand and watch
The next two go, wedged upside down between
The farmer's legs, to know
That somewhere in that ruffled sheen

My neighbour's knife had broken through
And watch the bird's panic and premonition ebb
As across their bright bead eyes
Slowly the coarse lids drooped and set.

Furtively, I shovelled soil upon the blood.
The children must not know or guess.
'It is the last time! Once is enough!' I said.
For hours I gathered up the incriminating fluff.

At the farm that afternoon another batch of cocks was bled.

WINTER IN WALES

*Each culture has its own new possibilities of self-expression which
arise, ripen, decay and never return . . .I see world-history as a
picture of endless formations and transformations of the marvelous
waxing and waning of organic forms.*
                    Oswald Spengler: The Decline of the West.

*My area, the Cardiganshire plateau, is ... basically a heath soil. It
was the hard work of men in the past that turned the plateau into
fertile farm soil. In my area we talk about a field 'going back'. This
means that some fields are not brought into rotation which is
essential to high farming and they revert to rushes.*
  Arthur Darlington. Taken from Proof of Evidence given to the Public
          Enquiry concerning the Mid-Wales Rural Development Board.

I walk among the ruined banks
Of Wales, through the charred hedges, wind-warped,
Over the snapped stalks, the withered grass,
And see upon the hill's bare skull
Phalanx upon phalanx of blades
Surrounding the farms with the white glitter of winter.

Returned to the low house, I recall
The autumn: the Mediaeval dance of Emperor butterflies,
The self-immolating flight of wasps,
The solitary swift, left by migrating flocks,
Which perched briefly on the frizzled branches,
Confounded by the cooling air - and then was gone.

At night I scan the sky:
Through the thick clots of darkness
A billion points of chilling light
Flash out. Flash out! And I imagine
The busy cities answering
With their neon-lighting, their clamorous factories
Welding steel to star, star to steel.

Unseen, corrugated leaves strike the empty roads
A world's undone. Flesh torn from the bones.
                    After Alexandria, Rome, the cold. After
London, Moscow, New York, the march
Over which
A blind wind moans.

PRELUDE

Where would you lead
    me and what
       would you have of
me, restless
    and enigmatic
       spirit? In
the enclosed garden
    it is again
       Autumn. Sycamore
leaves litter the
    small paths –
       the jagged leaves'
edges are turned
    inwards and everywhere
       their yellowness is
marred and blotched
    with blight. In
       the garden
the lemon light grows
    faint. Yet what
       are *you* doing
here, lover of
    strange mists and burning
       aromas,
at the open
    gate standing with
       the palms of your
hands showing? Will
    you wait - as
       I approach and
let me read and
    go where the lines
       take me?

THE WORD

You suggest and
provoke until
I chase -

chase you wherever
you will,
I would - but

where do you
go,
down which

turning, into
which
unused chapel of truth,

so many the turnings,
crosses,
ends, I do not know -

yet, tantalizer, how
can I
forget how

you beckon so, what
you would
pomise

in your lithe movement,
not to be mine,
grace

in my city,
out
of my power.

WHO WAS IT?

Who was it yesterday, at the window
Of my dark room,
With a young girl's lips
Incanting a language sweeter than honey,
Arms yellow as laburnam flowers
And with long delicate fingers
Lifted, and, for one moment, beckoning ?

And why did I, in an age worn through
With too much doing not follow?
Why did I turn back
To my desk, to shuffle again
This pale pack of abstractions,
Familiar and dead,
With only myself to deal to ?

And what, as I turned over
First archaic Queen, then King,
Was that sudden sensation
As of a cloud passing.
A shiver of breath.
A stillness. And on my forehead -
The clammy touch of death ?

THE SACK OF LEARNING

I

Outside Rome, tonight, the barbarian
Camp-fires are bright, ablaze
With ancient manuscripts.
Above the scattered tents,
Scorched with a new image
Of Faith become savage,

The red flags swirl
And whip the stars.
Inside the city walls,
Sent by indignant powers,
Thirty thousand troops rape,
Murder, burn and mutilate.

It has happened all
Before : the rueful acts,
Inclement crimes. Turbulence
Joining turbulence to call
Out the asylum of the mind,
Untether the straddling animal.

But all is well:
For pious men with shaven heads,
Stabling their horses in looted shrines,
Know their Divinity is free
To upend *idolatrous times:*
Annihilate ornate history.

2

A prisoner in Castel Sant Angelo,
Pope Clement strolls,
Long hair and beard,
Against the darkness quoting Job.

3

In one brief night
By Lutheran and lout

The giant tap-root of the mind
Pulled out :

The tree's fabulous foliage -
Set alight.

4

On the brow of the hill
Where clouds raise
And erase
Themselves and streams begin,
Watching, stand this King and Queen.
Immortal and primordial
They seem
To gaze upon the distant edge of things,
The morning's mist that might be mellow
With the sun's splay of light
Now blotched with smoke,

As from all sides, flames
And further flames encroach.

ESTRANGED

And what for that matter is a world but a mode of consciousness.
Kathleen Raine.

And now we spend our lives staring through these small
Windows, streaming with rain, salt-stained.
Out where we look little's to be understood;
Bucked by the wind, the hawthorn's branches twist all ways -
Their clustered berries bleed into the wood.
In the smudged glass Gwastod's barn is cut away
And the slang's flange's ruts reveal few variations.
Strange that we should share the same meal,
Be so near, yet feel estranged, both staring out.

Tonight as we lie in bed, a battered moon drifts
Through the sky - it seeks a glistening eye,
It seeks a low-tide pool, a mountain lake,
In which to dip its wounded face,
Its scarred distended cheeks, its frozen mouth.
Who will return its former life ? Its lost being ?
Its ancestral bearings ? Who will lend the slack night
The great curved mirrors of his mind
To house this nomad face ? We turn away.

We dream back to back. Toss restlessly.

INTO THE DARK

From time into
time,
into time, no
thing
survives.

Tonight as we touch
our hands are cold.

Wind levels. And
levels. And to whatever monuments, the clock
tocks :
pyramids in time are sand, sand desert.

Our limbs weigh
with the weight of centuries -

while love's elusive child rushes
into the dark,
scattering
his bold red fire.
Into
the dark.

We die as
we whisper.

And what things remain
mould,
go slowly
into this desert of slow
wind lulling forever
desert.
Desert.

Tonight our bed is passion's coffin.
Cold.

Dust settles.
Love. Universe. Poem.
Still.

And old.

WITHOUT WORDS

For hours now, for days, half
Dumb, three quarters
Dazed, I have stumbled round this place
Impotent to spin, from
The open book
To the vase of flowers,
From the room's cool shadow to
The incandescent pools of light shimmering
On the window sill,
The image web. Intending and
Willing, yet powerless
To unspool the locked word threads.

Outside I observe how the nettles
Slip hot tongues
Through the stones' hard armour,
Hoist beneath their own snapped stems green
Flags of resurrection.
Buds notch the sycamore boughs.
Small rhubarb crowns unfold their first
Furled leaves, tiny
And wrinkled as babies' hands.

I analyse them all,
Enviously!
Dense nature's endlessly recurring transformations.
And all day circle this lonely ward,
My last enclave, where - without
Words, without a world –
I lumber down the long dark corridors
Dividing bright domains.

ON AN UNTAKEN PHOTOGRAPH

I might have taken a photograph of you
Just now, kneeling in Brechfa's garden,
Holding up the new root of gypsophila,
Its limp limbs lifeless after so long a journey,
A thin goddess hovering above her mandrake,
Framed by the wall I built, pear trees we staked,
But such a picture would have been a fake,

A show-piece image for suburban evenings.
It would not have incarnated what we know -
How further down, beneath reaching of the spade,
Nettle and couch mat and burrow,
Ready to encroach - if we but pause or go -
Upon the paths and flowering borders, thrust
Through the eluding order we have laboured for.

Nor could you catch on celluloid the claws
Of shadow perched in the garden's cracks
And corners or show how imperceptibly they darken
As they slowly unclasp, arch further forward.
Ourselves, we barely sip the tip of what
We know - as now we merely remark
How cold it grows. Seem anxious to go in.

WHAT, YOU ASK, IS INTENTIONALITY?

for Barbara

What, you ask, is intentionality?
Consider our new-born son:
A small bundle of cuddled flesh,
Barely a fledgeling,
Yet between sucks darting into his mother's eyes,
Returning, vibrant
After such flying,
Thrusting his legs all ways: and smiling.

Or consider the flight of birds:
How, today, we saw the cormorant fly,
Its long neck stretched
Low to the incoming tide –
Where his eye lives.
Or take the mallard,
How, migrating by strange powers,
It shakes its wings
To the distant pattern of the stars.

Or take Man, Creator of Patterns,
Venatum Formarum! How
The trembling notations of Beethoven
Vault the darkness.
How in writing, the pouncing mind -
Its whole body dances up like flame -
Throws out a flash
Of light across the world,
Illuminates what it must catch.

What, you ask, is intentionality ?
Water pressed by flood
Spumes over stone.
These leaps of life: the fluttering rhythms

Of child and bird, the ache of love,
The seeking word take us on a wave
Arching forward into time.
We live by our intentions
Out of reach, beyond ourselves.

AFTER BAD WEATHER

This morning, after the year's weather's vagaries,
Wind's ructions, alternating day by day,
Salt-bearing storms, searing bud and foliage,
Grey corrugated days of drizzle rusting into rain,
I praise Nothing and walk the garden
Welcoming, as Autumn rotates into Winter,
The staring spaces, glinting gaps, white gashes.

Yesterday as we cut the old canes, snipping back
The brittle stems close to their dank source,
We watched the emptiness like released water flooding in,
Dart with bright expectant eyes, between the flapping
Leaves and severed stalks. And now as I recall
Our labour, I respond - I praise the constancy of space
Through which our world still meets and corresponds.

Against a tree's stark trunk our neighbour's ladder stands
Left from apple-picking. Its steel sides slant
Through the empty branches into a snow-cloud sky.
I notice, with strange pleasure, how through the geometry
Of silver rung, black bough, the clean light pours and
Water-falls. I go indoors, back to the day's routine, quietly
Holding in my mind's mirror gleaming images of futurity.

IT IS EVENING AFTER THE MAELSTROM

for the Darlington Family

It is evening, after the maelstrom,
After the upturning,
Burning and devastation of cities,
As reported on radio –
And (briefly) on television.
And prophesied in the last newspapers.

The herd stand by the farm's gate,
Dumb and enduring.
Even in this breeze, bitter
With mountain mist and drizzle,
Their ribbed flanks are calm as boulders –
Only their frayed tails twitching.

They have stood there
Ten thousand years, bulging
Eyes staring down
The dark track, trailing back
Through the charred centuries,
To the first spark of history.

Slathering, their warm breath
Wreathes the air; they await
Man's archaic canticle to cattle,
And a half-simple girl who wades
Slowly through the slang's
Slop and mud to guide them in.

The door opens on to dusty hay,
Bedding for a dozen animals.
Through the dark slates' cracks light
Needles the barbarian night -
Inside, at the finger's touch,
Thick milk drums into the pails.

FOR MAN AND ISLANDS

Today I walk the winter's beach, blind
To the flecked waves
Rising to the wind's pull,
Blind to beauty –
For the time's intolerant images
Storm my mind.

I see not waves but faces
Marching to the Age:
Faces numb with the cold wash of phrases,
Faces frozen with slogans,
Eyes swollen to flashing discs,
Minds hardened by helmets.

Between the waves the crowds surge
Hedgehogged with hurtling glass.
Dark blood tars the shore.
I see a child without limbs,
His arms blown to spray.
One bent hand floats like a claw.

I look out to sea and pray
For man and islands. I think of
Skellig Michael. Iona. Lindisfarne.
I see their jagged foreheads
Gazing back, their clenched fists
Raised above the water -

And I pray that their black-cracked rocks
Be ready to hold the storm-borne
Seeds again, to shield whatever
Fragile spores of hope may -
Though our times seem sterile - fall,
Be there to cradle what is new, once more.

WINTER SOLSTICE

And so we enter the dark hours of the winter solstice.
Lime green lichen seeps down the damp walls of this house.
The day sags like a farmer's sack hung out to dry.
Clouds, trees, grass, stare back, blank and immobile.
Even the sea presses on its bed of bladderwrack and weed,
Lifeless as a hunk of quarried stone.
And the small life of this cramped village continues as usual.

I listen to the wind. Its long blades cut
Through the corrugated sheds and shacks that wound these fields.
It brings to this chimney insubstantial lamentations,
Sounds that flock and beat their charred wings
Like memories released from caves and catacombs,
Too dark and distant to possess a name
Yet scrape the bone beneath the skin.

I will not listen to them, the wind's wailings, the dark voices,
The frozen underside of the burning sun.
We turn on the news again and watch
The tail-end of a civilisation slide and twitch
In the dust, determined neither to retreat nor run.
I look outside. Starless and drizzling the night hangs.
I confront my absurd quest - nothing achieved, nothing done.

BRECHFA

Bearing torn leaves, wrenched twigs,
From the shorn wood
The wind has come against our home.
Down these black cavernous chimneys
It has jabbed its harsh fingers
Wanting what was once its own:
And through every crack and rusted keyhole
Thrust its long knife blades.
And shuddered in the window-sills.

And, foolishly, we had undone the small
Improvised defences of wiser generations,
Wrenched from holes and hidden ledges
The cobwebbed rags, the matted wool;
And pulled from the door's edges
The thin hardboard slats
Nailed far into the rotting wood.
And in the garden burnt them.

And yet, again, this long Welsh house
Has held its ground.
Its slated roof, its mud-bound walls,
Its quarry tiles still stand, sound
And unbroken. Like Nature's shell, it shelters
Whatever scrap of life should enter
Seeking its own rhythm and pattern.
And now its doors and windows open
To a gentler morning.

In the garden, bracken fronds unfurl
Their cool heraldic beauty.
On old land between old walls,
My tongue feels free to move and praise
A rush of moments which,
Beyond all reason,
Now swell and shake like buds,
Shadowing the house in this green season.

from

SONGS OF A NEW TALIESIN

1981

THIS NOMADIC GOD

I
When the God was born on the hill we stayed inside.

II
When we spotted in the valley his bloody caul making the stream all red
Somewhat repelled, we walked away.

III
When on the same night we stared into his great eye
Glaring through our window we switched off the light;
We said: 'There can be no such thing.
Not in our times, 2000 Anno Domini.'

IV
When in the darkness he dared to rise through the basement of our house
We fumbled for the light and cried: 'Ah! Dreams! – and their archaic remnants.'
For we had read the literature. And sighed, relieved.

V
Later, when the trees' leaves shriveled yellow -
Later, when the bent bracken bled profusely -
Later, when the low snow clouds shed their icy shingle -
Later, when the white river no longer flowed but lay nailed to its own bed -
If you remember – and to be fair – we were both rather busy;
There were forms to sign, bills to clear,
And the house – it stood in constant need of attention and repair.

VI
Yet still the conjuror-god casts his signs about,
Daily scrawls his ikons on the shifting sands
Above reeling cities brushes his gentle ideograms
On concrete slabs executes his reckless graffiti.

VII

And still, on random days, he knocks on our locked door
Many times. Incisive knocks. Insistent. What would he have of us?
This trickster salesman, this nomadic god? If we let him in,
Would he annihilate our private space?
At our table does he want a simple place?
Is it that he wants a glass of wine? A slice of bread?
Two stale lives to transubstantiate?

THE TREE OF KNOWLEDGE

And in the cool of the evening
    the great God
        slept
satisfied. And in the tree's
    shadow
        Adam
drew close to Eve and knew
    her for
        the first
time and in the darkness of
    touching her
        his tongue,
adept as ever, adamant,
    rhapsodic,
        named her,
proclaimed her. And Eve held
    with awe
        love's
sticky stem till its nodding bud
    burst into
        flower, burst into
seed, deep, deep inside her. A high
    tide, their
        sighing
filled the whole garden. And
    subsided. Then
        one body
drawing the same breath, they dreamt
    the first
        dream
as they slept. The serpent uncoiled,
    rehearsed
        the next scene.

II
In the morning Eve woke
        to take
                the serpent's
apple. And walking through
        the garden
                she moved
elated, loving more and more the taste
        of her single
                self, self –
created. Querulous, she returned
        to Adam:
                'In love
Who is who? I'm not myself
        when I'm in
                you and who
are you when you're in me?
        Love's condition
                is not
free.' Adam took the fruit
        and both advanced
                to suffer
love's dilemmas. Alone, they desired
        to be together;
                together
they conspired to be apart; they met
        to squabble,
                parted
to idealise. Painfully they unlearnt
        each other,
                no longer
sure if hate might lie beneath
        the smile
                or love
behind the grimace. Could not
        accept or
                yet
escape what both half-

      ached for,
         half -
repudiated. The apple-bite became
      the love-bite.
         That night
restless, apart, they dreamt the second
      dream. The serpent
         left
the fading tree, slid into the dark,
      the garden closed –
         imperceptibly.

      III
God woke appalled, mind somehow
      dismembered,
         body,
somewhere bleeding, groped into
      a future
         He had not
foreseen, could not recognise.
      Divided, the lovers
         crawled
out from His dream, held
      firm His
         arms flailing
all ways. Locked together, lurching
      forwards and backwards
         and sideways,
they left dark stains on trees,
      on rocks;
         at every cross
and turning left crimson tracks.
      At the small
         gate
into history, a limping god slumped
      upon two mortal
         backs.

THE RETURN OF THESEUS TO ARIADNE

Tradition falsifies. I did not slay the minotaur.
It is true holding Ariadne's twine I descended
The black and airless labyrinth and, true,
That at a great depth I found the creature
Steaming in its own filth. Its two eyes
Like slits cut in the black back of matter
Examined me. I shouted *Minotaur !* and, at once,
We engaged in a heroic battle, in the pose
The story tellers clamour for. Yet that embrace
Was my undoing. Holding him in my hands
I lost the appetite to kill. He became
A murky mirror in which I glimpsed myself:
His slit eyes, I knew, were mine, blind
In the darkness of my own mind; his limbs
Urged me to sense the contours of my own body,
Amoral source of things. Even his grunts
Stirred memories down so deep I could not
Fathom them. So I lost the will to slay him
And, in the end, breathless, after much blood, we made
Our pact:I would daily descend to feed him
And, in return, though loath, he agreed to learn
My symbols. Dazed, I returned slowly, holding
The twine, the single strand, faithful to the end.
And at the cave's entrance Ariadne held me,
Caressed my torn flesh, kissed my sores;
She did not avert her eyes but with such love
Received all I had brought from the minotaur –
Who, as we lay, far below us, settled.

GOOD FRIDAY POEM

And on the Friday
Mary Magdalene
Came to her Christ,

Hung on the cross,
A noble bird,
Stripped of his plumage,

His white skin
Ripped, his quivering wings
Pinned to the wood,

And she lay with him
And in his great pain
He made manifest his love.

And on the next day
The bloody tree
Burst into bud

And migrating flocks perched
On the outstretched arms.
And there was song.

APHRODITE'S FLOWER

A rose is not a rose
is not a rose –
but the blossom is the free
spray of blood
shed by animals
on heat for Aphrodite.

The stem is not a stem
is not a stem
but a hooked chain
quick to claw
the hand straining
for possession.

The bud is not a bud
is not a bud –
but the crimson bed
of woman, red folded in
upon red, impregnating
the night with possibility.

The root is not a root
is not a root –
but a god's long phallus
underground, drilling
the darkness down and down
with dionysiac joy.

A rose is n6t a rose
is not a rose –
but the root, the bud,
the stem, the flower,
the incarnation of desire
spiked with briars.

TALIESIN THROUGH THE SEASONS

Wyv cerdoliad; wyv saer mal dryw
I am a musician - an artificer like the wren.

Inside the cycle
I dance and I dance.
I am Taliesin,
Master of trance.
Moulder of patterns
Remembrancer.

An artificer like the wren.

It is winter. It is dawn.
Upon the frozen dead
A flint rain falls.
The river's turbulent flow
And undulation's over –
Flat as a gravestone
Slab it lies; all that was
Living, stiff and brittle,
Gripped within it.

I am Taliesin.
I dance a slow dance.

Comes the spring, ice snaps
And cracks, the river
Groans through gaps;
The long locked water
Seeps up like poetry.
In a bright light
Cobwebbed with shadows
The world traffics in ice-floes.

I am Taliesin
I dance and I dance.

It is summer and noon.
Under the burning stone
Blanched roots splay out,
Restless as antennae,
Restless as life.
Eyeless, though the warm
Earth, the worm
Winds to the light.

I am Taliesin.
I dance and I dance.

Autumn comes, comes the dusk.
Christ hangs from
Every tree - His side split
Like a bursting husk.
His drops of blood
Are the leaves
Pouring down.
They sear the ground.

I am Taliesin.
I dance a sad dance.

Inside the cycle
I dance and I dance.
I am Taliesin,
Master of trance.
Moulder of patterns.
Remembrancer.

An artificer like the wren.

from

ICONS OF TIME

1991

PROLOGUE

I have searched for myself.
Heraclitus

I

A COSMIC STORY

And now, feeling querulous, God said *Let*
There be consciousness. And slept. And out
Of his long dream confused man stepped,
Scorched victim of divine fission.
Crazed animal dipped into time.
And under the mushrooming cloud and through
The black snow crept towards the crime
Of his history, immolating his own kind -
For there was this burn and ache in his side
Which nothing, for long, could assuage or cool.
Nor could he recognise that darker face,
Reflected back from the cracked world's pool.
And God woke from his dream. And half-understood.
Sensed the nails through the palms. And the chafing wood.

II

RETURNING TO SHERINGHAM

I walk the promenade. Half-familiar faces
Drift past me, so much less monumental
Than I remember, so badly cracked. And faded.
In their canvas tents the same women
Sit. Still. Knitting. Staring out.
A brackish wind blisters the day. I go
Up the steps to our old house - how it
Has shrunk! Under the salt-laden breeze paint
Has peeled. Black cracks in the wood are deeper.
Hedge and gate have been wrenched out to make
A parking space. Now only a summer-house -
Vacant half the year. How did we ever
Live here cocooned is such a claustrophobic place?
Across geometric lawns unknown children shout.

III

WAITING FOR THE HARVESTER

Here I stood in the crew-cut stubble,
Sharp stone in hand waiting for the harvester
To turn upon the final strip of wheat,
To see the hares dart wide-eyed into the gun's
Explosion or rise like crimson rags upon
The blades. Now, near the same spot I can
Hardly recognise the self I was;
Now I am no longer armed - I move
Across the earth, mesmerised; myself
Trapped in the last small track of wilderness.
At every footfall, at every dog bark,
Every quiver of the vast machine, I shudder.
Sense in my flesh my own sharp stone;
The damp blades whirring above dry bone.

IV

A FURTHER VISIT: FEBRUARY 1990

For my Mother

Back - and at each glance the town contracts.
How dwarf the buildings seem that once towered
Over me. All close-ups then; and sticky palms.
We take the bitter route along the promenade.
You talk of the latest deaths, lives slowly
Extinguished, last words said. At each return
There are further casualties to add. The sea
Is out; the iron defences bleed an oxide red.
At the cemetery we clear the grave. You plant
A rose. I touch the stone, sense Father's back;
White. Emaciated. Cold. A frenzied wind
Tears at our throats. The driven clouds blacken
The sun. I kiss you from the moving train.
The scene blurs behind me. It begins to rain.

V

ABSENCE

I have been here before, chest pressed
Against the stone's worn ledge, feeling the same
Unease as I do now, peering through the gloom
And silence to the abrupt stop of water.
Through the darkening clouds, criss-cross of boughs,
My face stares back. Mouth bearded, wrinkled brows.
An actor's mask whose parts I do not recognise,
Whose lines I can no longer read. Hamlet
Without an audience? More like Narcissus -
Only myself here, under alternating focus.
What did I, a child, throw down this well?
A gap exists where the syntax ends.
There's a numbing sense of loss. Nothing
Comes back. This silence where these shadows toss.

VI

WHO I AM

He did not observe that with all his efforts he made no advance -
meeting no resistance that might, as it were, serve as a support upon
which he could take a stand, to which he could apply his powers,
and so set his understanding in motion.

Kant

What is it that I do? This dizzy spinning
Of myself. This geometric cobweb that I make
From my own entrails. Intractable substance,
Obsessively shaped to a fine thread.
Part fact. Part fabulation. An obscure agent
In me fashioning the dark strands into pattern.
A design, somehow redemptive, however difficult.
What was could not have been otherwise.
There's a kind of freedom in admitting it.
Facts are weights. They tether random flight,
The delusions of Icarus, the Romantic type.
Filament by filament, inch by inch, I make
This architecture: a bound and limited life.
What I have struggled with is who I am.

FRAGMENTS FROM A CATHOLIC CHILDHOOD

I rhyme
To see myself to set the darkness echoing
Seamus Heaney

I

PREMATURE BIRTH

<u>Surname</u>: Abbs. <u>First names</u>: Peter Francis.
<u>Date of birth</u>: 22.2.42. <u>Place</u>: Cromer.
The facts console. Deceive and mesmerize.
Yet mother's story has a nightmare ring.
All the way to the theatre she had screamed:
I want to die, I want to die, I want -
Until the gas took over. Born premature –
Cut from the womb three months too soon -
I choked into the commotion of hands, the glare
Of swivelling lights, muffled blare of plenitude.
Mother sighed *A girl? A girl?* and bitter, wept.
For her: scars from the surgeon's knife.
For me: slow, impeded waking into life.

II

AT THE OAK WOODS

This morning, not as it usually is.
Not box-hedge, nor black currant, nor mint's aroma.
Merely the breeze tapping the window pane -
And Grandmother's there. With pins, with clips, she plaits
Her hair. Grandfather's sipping tea from his saucer.
I've slipped the intervening years again.
On the fire branches froth, sizzle, blaze, smoulder.
The varnished chairs shimmer like manufactured glass,
Their curving legs are tongues of fire.
I go down the green passage to the open door,
Splinters of God lie in the melting grass.
The marigolds stand erect, orange and oracular.
I go through the walled garden to the pond.
A goldfish surfaces. Circles. And is gone.

III

IN THE WOODSHED

In the corner of the garden was the shed.
Across the door a fig tree arched, and spread.
Warmed by the sun its ribbed fruit hung down;
A ripe purple stained the outer rind.
Yet the palmate leaves were hands prohibitive;
They joined to shut one out. When pushed,
The door swung open. Inside it was illicit
Dark. Chill underground. I paused - time passed -
Then tiptoed down. Slowly they materialized:
In a corner kindling limbs were stacked and bound.
Serrated teeth gleamed from each black side.
A hacked torso rose up from the ground.

A nightmare rides rough-shod upon my sleep.
I was in too far. And down too deep.

IV

MYRTLE COTTAGE AT WEST RUNTON

The West Runton Abbs were Methodists.
They ate meat on Fridays, placed no crucifixes
On the mantelpiece, read *Pilgrim's*
Progress and *The Methodist Recorder. Papists*
Grandmother spits out the word like it burns
Her mouth. Grandfather keeps himself apart.
Where the coast road turns to Roman Camp
He sits on the village bench. And talks Socialism.
I don't believe in any God you dress
Up for, he says. *And read between the lines!*
All his life he laboured for the genteel classes
He most despised. In Myrtle Cottage
A wood fire glows. Dark above the old bureau
An antlered stag stands high, where water flows.

V

THE OTHER CHILD

I look through the window of my first school:
St Josephs. R. C. Sheringham. Norfolk.
Through the pane of fractured glass I stare
Into that silent chamber, sunk from mind.
Silver radiators still stand by the dark green
But all the trappings - abacus, globe,
Charts, blackboard, maps - have long since gone.
Was I ever here? Learning God by rote?
Obscure eel in the shallow tank of learning -
Even then forgetful of names, dates, facts.
I cannot find the child I was. Nothing
Coheres. Or coincides. Or rhymes.
The school door's locked; the place is out of bounds.
A pensive boy inside does not turn round.

VI

ST PETER'S COLLEGE FOR CATHOLIC VOCATIONS: 1954

I mourn the child I seldom was. Precarious
At birth. Washed up, at last. At St Peter's
College. Freshfields. Liverpool. A pale
Face elongated with piety. Alabaster
Hands clutching the plastic beads. Or clasped
Before the fourteen Stations of the Cross.
Baroque actor straining to shed the child
Who seldom was. Who cried himself to sleep
While the Mill-Hill fathers' red sashed cassocks
Cracked and slapped against our wooden cells.
And priests in black gowns were walking their rounds
And binding with briars my joys and desires.

Dear child, I would tell you if I could.
A stricken deer makes for the shadowed wood.

VII

THE ECZEMA OF CHRIST

I remember your raw hands, first. And now
I see your face. Scored red. And white with flaking.
The eczema of Christ! And your name? What was your name?
Was it Bailey? Slowly you said something
Like: *Go to the Loaches…. It's the best place.*
It stank of excrement. But you were right.
The blocked homesickness streamed down my face.
That night I watched the Liverpool-Southport
Trains glide by. Each lonely passenger glowed
With a freedom I conferred upon them.
Mundane life - that lost beatitude!
On Friday nights we confess on bended knees.
We scour our soiled imagination clean.
A sick Christ dangles from the plastic beads.

VIII

AN UNDELIVERED LETTER

Oh, but Christ, you were hooked on prayer.
Your cocaine rosary, your litany of valium,
Your cheap narcotics always at hand,
Available whenever the going got rough -
Or our exams came. Hunched in the church,
Small hands barricading your face, lips
Pursed up against the world's violation.
All that sacrifice! All those prayers! -
As the day-trippers mobbed past outside.
We felt we could not turn Cliff Road
Without the intercession of the Saints.
And I, ham actor, sick to please
Tried to outstrip the illustrious saints for years,
Addicted to the dark, violet, heart-shaped words.

▼

IX

THE DEATH OF GRANDMOTHER 1960

I was eighteen when Grandmother died.
She had fainted at the Catholic fete.
Was deep in a coma when we reached her side.
She recognised none of us.

Our agitated words sink into silence.
Your face hangs a crumpled mask come loose;
Somewhere your life edges into blackness;
The beads I give you dangle like a noose.

And she who filled our lives with so much talk
Died alone without a single word.
I look at you now in your wedding photograph;
Demure. More beautiful than I remember:

Any second your mouth will burst into a smile.
Your animal eyes hungry for their future.

X

IN THE MUSEUM

Unceremoniously they lay that ancient
Body out, unwrap the limbs. One by one,
Peel back the binding resin rinds.
With scalpels cut the pad of chaff and mud.
They number every bone. Brush, weigh and pack
The crumbling aromatic dust; unstring
The pious tags and take the last frail sheaves
Of faith, centuries of hope, dissolving.
Yet what do these masked surgeons work
To find under the scents and gnostic tricks
Of Anubis? Naked on the block
A human mortal lies: H7386;

Her hollow head, tilted back, rapacious
Mouth open, still gagging on the nothingness.

XI

THE LOSS OF FAITH

What did we do when we unchained the earth from its sun?
Are we not plunging continually?
Are we not straying as through an infinite nothing?

Nietzsche

Who put the neon-lighting of his childhood
Out? A juke box throbs with *Jail House Rock*.
He reads Karl Marx and dreams of freedom.
He smooths his hair with daubs of Brylcream.
Gone from the Eucharist, where is God?
On Sheringham sands *I can connect nothing*
With nothing. The spray lashes into the dark.
In my own town I have become a stranger.
I kneel and pray before the blessed virgin –
My mind's a stew where Magdalene strips.
I enquire of all that lives its final aim.
The ornate dome of faith cracks and splits.
God created the world *ex nihilo*. And withdrew.
Then, one day, the nothingness seeped through.

FATHER AND SON

Spirit gains its truth only by finding itself in absolute dismemberment

Hegel

I

TONGUE-TIED

Father, now when I speak, I speak for you.
The silence you maintained could not be kept.
A knife, it spliced our mutual lives in two.
Tongue-tied, we were forever awkward. And inept.
Silence was our dumb inheritance.
The suicidal note passed down to us:
Keep your tongue still. Keep your mouth shut -
Numbing contract of our rural class.
The laconic words were slowly drawled
To dam our thoughts and let the feelings pass.
Nothing. Say nothing. Say nothing at all.
The anger mounting in the throat was swallowed back;
And swallowed back it became all hell to know
What the dumb thing was which choked us so.

II

CONFIDENCE IN SPEAKING

In your wardrobe there were some pamphlets;
Their covers were crimson, the paper textured. *Smart,*
Mother would have said, with their striding titles:
CONFIDENCE IN SPEAKING IN TEN EASY PARTS.
But for us there was to be little confidence.
No public. No easy parts. The blade of silence
Axed whatever lived between us. *Life's*
A fucking swindle if you ask me, you said once.
But I didn't really ask. So the years passed.
Quietly they incinerated themselves.
Unremarked those crimson invitations
Disappeared. Tonight, because you're ill, I phone.
We cannot find the words we need, our speaking parts.
Our voices falter. That age-old silence starts.

III

LANGUAGE!

Father, what was it which divided us?
It crawled without a name. It grew in our
Embarassment. A freak. An albatross
Worn privately. Yet it came from a power
Outside. *The 44 Education Act. The new welfare.*
This weekly drama comes drifting back.

My brother has returned from Paston School.
He does his language homework in the parlour;
Declines regular nouns, corrects bad grammar.
Father, you scan *The Mirror* on the kitchen stool:
Jesus Christ! The bitch went down! Bloody Hell!
Fucked up m'bleedin Vernon's Pools as well!

Language! Language! Language! I hear my mother gasp.
The curtains hang like iron across the glass.

IV

GENERATIONS OF FARM HANDS

A metal sky weighs upon the horizontal land,
Drained, dyked, undemonstrative.
After all these years, I work to understand:
Give the silence a voice, the resentment tongue,
To brand it indelible on the fugitive mind.
Where did it begin, that subterranean anger,
Smouldering, barely exploding, quickly subsiding?
Chill ash. The lava of embarassment.
Was it being born rural working-class?
Generations of farmhands, time out of mind,
Forcing their feelings down till they drowned
To resurrect, embittered, against their own kind.
Civilization's dismemberment of man. Not hearts.
Not heads. Not tongues. But hands, severed hands.

V

PREDICAMENT

Father, what was it made us quell our convictions?
Tame our moving tongues? We had no politics.
No public thoughts. Our feelings became convicts
Without right of expression. Tortured by shame
They couldn't announce themselves in the boisterous
Square nor exonerate their names.
We hadn't the heart to claim the beauty of anger.
The pride of justice. Whatever truth stirred
In our shallow lives we hammered down.
Daily, we slew our aspiring selves and deemed
It wise. *Well, who the fuck does he think he is?*
Too clever by half!
Cut him down to size!
Yet all the time the bitter sea spoke otherwise.

VI

WRITTEN IN GUILT

Father, even before the cards were cut,
Shuffled and dealt you said: *Count me out.*
At Mass your mouth shut tight as a clam
You crawled up the side-aisle to your god,
As if communion was all presumption
On your part or, more like, some *fucking sham.*
I analysed your Christian gestures with an adolescent
Eye which had become, by then, savagely
Unchristian. Father, why did you have to go
Leaving not one sign, not one memento?
What was it jammed the body's flow?
You looked on, spectral, awkward, half-ashamed,
And craved extinction years before it came.

And who can forgive me now for saying so?

VII

AFTER RETIREMENT

And so, your retirement came. A short speech.
A drink or two. A few quid in an envelope.
Then there was no more spiel - or tips.
No further excursions billed MYSTERY TRIPS.
At night as the ecstatic sagas flowed
You crouched coughing up gobbets of phlegm.
Death sat sour on the grave of your tongue
And in a claustrophobic room with flowers
Time's demolitions haunted you. The decades,
Years, months, weeks, days, hours
Dissolved to this consuming now - to disappear.
Beyond the mock-Tudor windows could you hear
The despotic sea, wind perpetual, drift of things?
The stopped clock, clogged, under tidal sands.

VIII

WINTER VISIT

Day staggers in, glazed-eyed, an invalid.
Morning contracts to shrunken appetites.
Little endures that interests you much.
Something like tears slide down the glass.
Your allotment, hard won, reverts to wilderness.
The fertile square is now couch grass.
Downstairs the chiming clock conveys a measured
Sense of things, not our snapped thread
Where beads in darkness scatter out of reach -
Under the silent bed. Under the silent past.
Nothing culminates. I walk the beach -
The Bingo's boarded up, the glass pane's smashed.
I sidle the length of my childhood cage.
An empty bench observes the breaking waves.

IX

A CONVERSATION WITH THE DOCTOR AT THE TIME OF THE CHERNOBYL DISASTER

You stand at the window in your striped pyjamas,
Like a disaster victim, and I am outside.
It is the second of May. The hawthorn blossom
Froths and blows all over Sheringham.
The doctor takes me to his car and says:
Your father hasn't much longer to go.
Over our heads the arctic clouds explode.
And mushroom. *He has the worst heart I know.*
The wind, unseen, plucks at our hair and clothes.
He is living on borrowed time. And pills.
I catch you at the window waiting for news.
There is nothing; nothing more medicine can do.

You turn to me, taciturn: *What did he say?*
And all about us spreads cancerous May.

X

CRISIS

As a child destroys a toy it has become
Indifferent to, so nature has it in for you.
Once partisan, now it doesn't care a jot;
It knows precisely where, when, how you'll crack.
The plastic bottles untidy the tidy house.
You swallow pills for urine, pills for gout,
Pills for sleep and now tranquilisers to ease
The dying. For two days they knock you out.
You drift among us, neither living nor dead.
Then the waves of pain come surging back;
They break over your hallucinating head.
All night you drown for want of common breath.
Day washes up the mess. Nothing's to be done.
A holocaust sky blots out the sun.

XI

NOVEMBER GARDEN

This November's slow. An aging sun weeps cold
On stone. You remain an invalid in bed.
Your body's shrunk. You lie small as a child.
I won't fucking mend this time, you said.
Your mind meanders through a maze its own.
The clinical air blasts my face and head.
And all you want is to be left alone.

This garden's become a place I almost dread.
A rectangle of smoking foliage. More gaps
Than substance. What fruit remains is cut and hollow.
The weight of barren years drags down my steps.
I recall early frosts, the drifting snow,
Snow that, once, as we walked, filled in our tracks –
Snow that was always driving in, behind our backs.

XII

OTHER MEMORIES

Father, I've been unjust to you.
Less than fair. Large with my own self.
Janus, the two-faced god, is always true;
There were other times. We had other selves.
Now I remember how in slippers you padded
To our room, to turn out the gas light.
The small gashed globe went ember-red
And briefly smouldered on into the night.
As the purring faded our room regained
Its attic silence. And then you quietly came
To both our sides. You made the sign of Christ
Upon our sleepy heads. And said 'God bless'.
Now in the greater darkness, the small light out,
Your clumsy silent hands seem, almost, eloquent.

XIII

REQUIESCAT IN PACE

Words on the gravestone of Eric Charles Abbs

When we saw your body laid out, decked
By mortician's hands, mother kissed your lips -
As if you were breathing still - and merely slept.
But I sensed, most of all, an absence.
Your head was arranged like an effigy
In wax. Life-like - yet unlike you. So cold
To touch! Finally, you'd gone.
                                    Two years have passed.
I catch sight of you now in glinting mirrors.
In my own feelings identify your quirks of soul:
Restless. On edge. Depressed. Equivocal.
Nature's both angel and born terrorist.
She slaughters to continue. The self's like breath -
Ephemeral. Yet I'll find words for both of us.
Make poetry break and bear the silence.
Requiescat in pace.

XIV

FF11506 DRIVER

Those who suffer in silence know no history.
Plato had a metaphor for it. Blindness,
Passivity of mind. He put us underground,
Hunched prisoners of the dark, watching dark
Shadows cast upon the dark. Exiled from the sun.
An absence of light. And no clear lineage.
Given the tabloid version, the TV image.
The cavern's shadows were always on the screen.
We'd no idea of who we were or who we'd been.
We went ashamed of what was rightly ours.
When relations died we burnt their personal things.
The photographs melted in the ash like tears.

Today I come across your driver's badge;
I grab it like a kleptomaniac.

XV

THE SINGING HEAD

Harsh. And remote. A square for graves.
A mile from Sheringham. The coast road.
Wind warps the hawthorn. Dwarfs the pines.
Brine abruptly burns the memorial rose.
Mother mourns here, planting against the odds.
Over the inscribed slabs gulls rise and scream.
Singed petals scatter across the epitaphs.
The incoming sea's chopped white and green.

Orpheus' head churns in its own blood,
Shudders with each and every turbulence;
Battered, blind, it turns; bobs on the flood:
A severed head that will not sink,
But through the silence and the blood-stained rings
It sings - it sings - it sings - it sings - it sings.

AFFAIRS OF THE HEART

The least things in the universe must be secret mirrors to the greatest
De Quincey

I

THE ANCESTRAL VOYAGE

Tonight rain clouds hang over Morfa Mawr,
Stranded whale which slopes into the bay
Of Cardiganshire. Against the dry stone wall
Our long Welsh house rests like a boat - each small
Window signals amber - now ready to float
Out on the incoming, gradual, tide of night.
Already our two daughters are asleep.
Their feet, like cut quartz, jut from the sheets;
Blond hair tangled in a galaxy of stars.
Our small son jerks his wrinkled hands, stirs
Momentarily. Murmurs. Returns to dream
The ancestral voyage. I perform last rites;
Top up the falling fire, wind the clock's
Dead weights, slide the bolt across the door,
And slowly come to you. My love, once more.

II

BAD TIMES

The family thrives - but we divide time
Between Simenon and sleeping pills;
Our daughters, wide-eyed, flare through the house.
Play punk. Pout. Shout. Take possession.
They gaze in mirrors, lie without a blink,
Grab your underwear, grin, evaporate.
We move cautiously, avoid reflecting
Surfaces, keep cool, convey their messages.
Upstairs I struggle to thaw iced words;
You empty slops, iron, wash and shop.
Tranquillised we glide through Safeways, ghosts
Of our former selves. We wheel an empty box
Through frozen flesh and pyramids of tin -
Too far gone to see the hell we're in.

III

FEAR BEFORE THE SACRED GARDEN

See how the couple tread with caution -
For they intrude upon this garden where
All living species move through fire to fire,
Scarring the dumb earth, scorching the air.
See how in this uncompromising place
Even the cedar is half-conflagration -
The matted boughs crack and flare with spikes
Of light so sharp they end all concentration.
There is a meaning in their sombre dress,
The suburban lady's dark oppressive clothes;
Even the hat may form some kind of shield
Against the daemonic sun's hot hammer-blows.
Then are they wrong to turn, quickly retire
From this garden of apocalyptic fire?

IV

SUNDAY MORNING AESTHETIC

You sit at the edge of the table, nude; your flesh
So finely stretched the ribs and bones show through.
African girl I come to you through CD
Players, Mozart's arias, Beaujolais Nouveau;
Our Sunday morning aesthetic. You gaze
Wide-eyed at us, part of the Sabbath's kill:
A snap, a shot buried between CITROEN AX
And KAWASAKI ZX10. You look at us;
Having nothing to sell or to display
You are the pitiless zero from which we rise.
Behind your body and your staring eyes
The shutters are almost closed against the day.

Outside on the suburban lawn the starlings preen,
Pick their gaudy wings. Strut. And gleam.

V

LOVE'S BATTLEGROUND

How in this warring marriage to survive
Love's battleground? We drag through the detritus
Of our own making. In the debris
Nothing grafts or roots or grows between us.
Terrorists we alter tack from hour to hour.
Your eyes open like blades. They're quick to cut.
My mouth is loaded with words. They aim to kill.
This is a prolonged and quite immoral war.
We suspect each other; read for duplicity;
Expect the worst. Emotions crash through our negotiations:
Escaped children, patients, war-lords - all of them crazy.
Our apprehensive looks are their exhausted faces.
Now, for no reason, there's a reversal of mood.
We're kissing like adolescent kids.
An interlude.

MOVING OUT

*For all ego-consciousness is isolated; it separates and discriminates,
knows only particulars and sees only what can be related to the ego.
Its essence is limitation, though it reaches to the furthest nebulae
among the stars.*

Anais Nin

I

STARTING AGAIN

Momentarily a shadow rises on the rocks.
Then, as darkness devours the light, is gone.
A loose pebble leaps its scree. And drops.
Somewhere, blind bolts of water thunder down;
A crystal snaps and shivers the labyrinth -
Noise without narrative, sound without sense:
An ibex rears. A bison mounts. A muzzle shudders -
Lost to memory in the lapse of tense.
And then it starts. And starts again. In the dark
A hand rises up; splays out, imprints itself.
Flat *mappa mundi;* high on the rock,
Dripping ochre and white, stark sign of the self.
The lines materialize. The palm's pressure.
A map. To be read at desperate leisure.

II

EXCAVATION

*This sort of archaeology depends on the careful peeling off of
successive thin layers of earth over a large area. In this way the team
progress step by step towards the original surface. They move down
five centimetres at a time and as they go down they are, of course,
going further and further back in time.*

Richard Leakey

Down. And further down. Back. And back -
What I seek is so distant, buried so
Far down under the thin tissues of black
Sediment, under the bric-a-brac, below
The charred pathologies of bone;
Down through the streaming lava flow
Of things, petrified: pots, beads, cut stone,
Ochre, ikon, pollen, sheer debris - slow
Recalcitrant clues to another's living;
Down through the shards of crumbling years,
Remorseless archaeologist, peeling
Back, one by one, the eluding surfaces -
Mad to grasp in this god-forsaken place
Minute fragments of the primordial face.

III

VIA NEGATIVA

Once there had been this God. He melted on
My tongue. Mouth sealed, I sighed. I would
Preserve the taste of Him until the end
Of time! I pressed my palms against my eyes
Wanting the light more incandescent for
The darkness. A gawky teenager, not
Of his age, a cauldron of overheated
Appetites, desirous of martyrdom.
Still at the brink, restless, addicted
To more than life can yield, I set myself
To learn subtraction in this Edwardian home -
Where the unseen worm mines the antique wood.
There are small heaps of dust in every room.

I'm haunted by my own ingratitude.

IV

AT THE EXTREMITIES

This evening, under the tumultuous cloud, stubble
Burns, cracks and smoulders. The fields are stark
Rectangles of death. Flints glint from rubble
And furrow. Outstrips of chalk gash the dark.
Persephone drifts here,
Singed poppies limp in her scarlet dress,
Her drugged mind driven near
The sudden gap in things where Hades is.
And Tolstoy, restless, to the end
Passionate for horizons, tracked by cameramen;
At the last station of his half-cracked mind
Whispering: *I must go on. I must go on.*
And now a crescent moon drifts over the Downs -
Brief sign above glimmering boundaries.

V

AFTER FAITH

For some years I could not see. First faith
And faith's intensity blotted out my sight.
Then the ideal came. It spread a cataract
Across my eyes. Its harsh and minute scale
Became the boundary of a guarded world.
It blocked out the variegated life of things.
These summer fields, this mist, the tidal Ouse
Which slowly snakes through two chalk hills.
Prisoner of a paradox, I could not see
Through what I saw. My eyes were boarded in.
Today I head for Nature's holes and gaps.
My mind's out there, coinciding with whatever moves
Or simply is. Clouds merge with the evening haze.
The river's a small 's' between two mists.

VI

THE BUDDHA STATUE

On the Downs they are burning the stubble;
Across the fields smoke clouds rise and billow.
Stalks and husks are being burnt to dust -
Even the last thin silk poppies have to go,
Surrender their scarlet to the black. I linger
At the edges, to turn the cold dank shards
Of memory, to word a further question.
Yet on the mantlepiece the Buddha statue stands.
His crowned head is an infolded flower.
His slim body a stem in the jug of being.
His dark body glimmers.
All through the annihilating
Motion of this day his hands are still.
Time turns upon itself. And spirals in.

VII

OPEN TO CHANGE

Out from this rock, wind-worn, rain-razed
The Buddha stares into the bludgeoning storm;
The shrubs' roots crack open the dome of his mind;
The husks, bursting, break his woman's smile:
The death of the Buddha! And all patriarchs!
Yet he's composed; more tranquil now than when
His maker hacked him from intractable stone.
Soon blue butterflies will flit before him;
And ants will crawl across those worn eyelids;
By his shoulders the leaves will burst their calyx
And unfold. Green. Yellow. Shrivel. And fade.
Beneath his gaze our lives betray themselves:
Broken, open to change. And the world turns
And turns. And the light burns. And the light burns.

VIII

EPILOGUE POEM: THE APPLE

Through open lips the paradox flows;
The clown's laughter is a refraction of sorrow.

In writing this I've half erased my life.
I hear no voices. Have fewer memories now.
I buried a rectangular box last night.
The full moon was witness and participant.
After we had mourned my loss together
She moved on, a face, between the stars.
It was the clearest night I've ever known. Not a cloud.

I am what I apprehend.
What I have struggled with is who I am.

The cooling air eddies at my finger tips.
The apple on this branch is not yet picked,
Touched by moonlight, before perception split.

from

PERSONAE

1996

1

IT BEGINS

ARJUNA TO KRISHNA BEFORE BATTLE

Reveal thyself to me. Who art thou in this form of terror?

In flayed skins, a crown of skulls,
He came. A wheel of dread, divine

Terror trampling the ground.
North, South, East, West.

Partner to pandemonium,
Light of a thousand suns:

A city explodes. A slum ignites.
Splinters of glass scream into the face;

Time's mutant, a scrap of flesh,
Limps shrieking into no time,

Into no place. A thousand chants, prayers,
Mantras make no difference;

The thousand lives of the golden Buddhas
Make no difference. A thousand pilgrimages

To a thousand shrines, no difference.
Under the debris

A severed hand weeps for its arm.
Closer to cockroach or termite

God stomps in His shadow,
Death's impresario, death's doyen.

No beginning, no middle.
No end.

Thus Arjuna before Krishna,
In the Bhagavad Gita,

The eleventh book, dumb with awe,
His hair on end.

WHAT, GOD WILL YOU DO?

Developed from a conception of Rilke's

What, God, will you do when I am dead?
I am your vase. What if I am carelessly broken?
I am the clay vessel which carries your drink.

Where, God, will you be when I am dead?
I am your listening ears; I am your glancing eyes.
I am your tongue through which you taste your earth.

How will you mature when I'm not there?
For I am your evolving language. I stutter your conceptions.
I utter your immense feelings. I chart your meanings.

I'm your prayer. What will you do without me?
What will you do without your scribbling messenger?
Will you continue blind and alone?

God, I am your dramatist. When the play is over
I fear the silence and see only desert,
Where appalling winds rake the sand, for ever.

2

THE PHILOSOPHER INVESTIGATES

HERACLITUS SPEAKS

A lost fragment circa 500 BC

Thinking is a sacred disease

Society equals the triumph of appearance over meaning,
Of saying over seeing. So I keep myself remote,
Avoid the mob in the agora, political meetings,

And the like. I spend time in the Temple of Artemis;
Play draughts with the kids of Ephesus or patrol
The squalling shore North of the Cayster. The violence of the sea

Succours me: its arching waves, its drenching spray,
Its salty transience. Nature loves to hide -
But here I sense the fracas of opposites. Strife is justice:

Contraries are apposite. Yet the crowds crave subterfuge
And are estranged, while politicians postpone
Their lives for ribbons and rhetoric. Let us not conjecture

At random about the greatest things. Hour after ephemeral hour
I inhabit the circle of time, the circumference of fire.
Nature's sputtering mouth. Her multitudinous mirror.

XANTHIPPE'S NOTE TO SOCRATES CIRCA 399BC

I have provided myself with this wife, because I am quite sure if I can put up with her, I shall find it easy to get on with any other human being

> Socrates as quoted in
> Xenophon's Conversations of Socrates.

Point one. I finally and absolutely refuse
To answer any more of your excruciating questions.
Point two. I've lived with you for years
And am sick to death of that gadfly speech;
Never use it again when we have visitors.
And never try that stuff about maieutics
When your mother's here. It's damned insulting.
She was a real midwife. Not like some.
Three. If you believe reason can unpick
The threads of life then you're an even bigger
Block-head than I thought. When the strands
Hang separate, how can they compose the pattern?

Wisdom can be secured at the cost of life
And a man's virtue degrade his wife.

But in Athens what can any woman do?
I'll go down in history as your shrew.

DESCARTES' DREAMS

I resolved to make of myself an object of study.
And waited. Slowly the silt-stirred river of my senses
Settled. Now, as if in the heart of a desert,
I test earth's rudiments. I begin where I am.
I start alone. Behind the scented rose I deduce
God's geometry; beneath the bird's iridescence
The machinery of bone. I place this wax into the fire's flame:
Smell exhales. Taste evaporates. Colour goes.
What, then, was real in the aroma of the rose?

Then came dreams. Nightmares. Whirlwinds blew me
Off balance. Forced me to stagger. I limped on my left foot,
A cripple. I saw machines perched on earth
Their silver nozzles sleeker than birds' beaks, pointing upwards,
Glinting. In a glass metropolis of numbers
Under high silent clocks phantoms gathered.
And where the bland wax stood packs of food rose up
Odourless, frozen, coded. On the edge of a precipice
A black boy beckoned. Smiling, he offered me a melon.

I woke. I couldn't sleep, nor could I quickly free
My mind from its own spectres. Dawn returned
God's reason. The sun's circle is at my elbow; its light
Is on this desk. It glows upon my words to illuminate
Their geometry - these iron links, iron rivets,
Hammered and chained together in Frankfurt,
Neuberg, Rome, Paris, Holland. And tested
Over nine long years. I distrust the sleep
Of reason. My quest continues.

ECCE HOMO: THE BREAKDOWN OF NIETZSCHE 1889

Truth is an army of metaphors

I was crucified last year
And go everywhere in my student overcoat
I am God I made this caricature
This Autumn I attended my funeral twice.
Questions, like waves, explode in the brain.
Anonymous the tide returns. At the end
Of the century the quarry's unchanged. Deaf
To the words wrought from our disenchantment,
Sublime discontent, unimaginable morning
Erupts again. The ocean glints. Through a ring
Of callous blue the eagle hovers. And drops.
The blood drips on the silent rocks.
The words darken the page. *I am a clown*
Of the new eternities. I promise a tragic age.

HOMAGE TO SIMONE WEIL

*I didn't mind having no visible success but what did grieve me was
the idea of being excluded from that transcendent kingdom to which
only the truly great have access and wherein truth abides. I preferred
to die rather than live without that truth.*

Born miscreant, awkward, gauche, dropper of pens, bottles,
Indiscreet words in discreet places;
Deposer of ease, you scorched the smug with the beat
Of your aphorisms and cut subterfuge
With a dialectical knife. *The categorical imperative in skirts*
They said. And they were right.

Infallibly you sought the evergreen wood on the further side
Of suburbs, the frenzy of roads.
Feeling the dry bark of the trees in your nicotined hands
You could sense the sap's
Rise and flow. You beat the brambled paths - small, obscure,
Overgrown - and kept them clear.

In your nomadic life each disheveled flat became a cell
For the search. You rolled back
Carpets wanting your feet square on the wood. Where there was
So much evil, there had to be
Good. All night, insomniac, you stretched thought's syntax until it
snapped
Into the unspeakable glory of God.

And how well you knew our fragility. A connoisseur of affliction,
Only you could make migraine
A stratagem to vision. Then in the slums of Paris you picked Him
up without
Remorse or shame, the Wounded One -
The Logos of Blood and Vinegar - and, like a deported Jew,
Starved yourself to death in His name.

And so now they come to your pauper's grave. *Is this the way
To Simone Weil?* Saint of outcasts;
Heretic on all sides. *August 30th 1943. Age 34. French refugee.
Buried at six feet.* Author of *Gravity
And Grace.* Above the grass there's a porcelain blueness of air.
And light falling through space.

WITTGENSTEIN'S FURNITURE

Wittgenstein's furniture is all over the place.
His severe steel chair lies on its back;
The clean windows are blasted to smithereens.
The hands of time have been torn off. The clock
Ticks absurdly. It has a vacant face.

A formal note on the stripped floor reads:
The limits of my language are the limits

Of my world. Sheathed in sequins, the boy
Glides through the dazzling light, his hair
Silver and gold from speechless dreams.
Fifty feet up and more, his hands grip air
Before he returns to dive through his shadow

Effortlessly. Mesmerised, the spectators scream.
Bowing, unburnt Icarus leaves the ring.

3

THE PAINTER'S TESTIMONY

REMBRANDT IN WINTER

(The signature at the bottom of *Self Portrait Aged 63* has
disappeared except for the letter 't')

At sixty three what matters now?
Death deals her signs.
Yet an unfamiliar light coruscates your brow,
Gutters and shines.

At the bottom corner of the frame
The darkness floods.
Of your illustrious baker's name
The 't' still floats

For Transience and Time which engulf all
Desperate strokes.
I sign my name because I'm mortal;
Born to pass.

Stranger, I wanted you to know that once,
Hands clasped together,
I faced myself. And with no chains of office,
In ice-cold weather,

Without furs or velvet hat or bronze breast plate
In a brown coat,
In the failing heart of winter, worked to place
Against the deficit

Some positive: my mind - mind's reflection - myself
At every move,
Watching experience unravel itself
Down to the spool.

ARTEMESIA GENTILESCHI

I want to show you, illustrious sire, how a woman can paint.

I am Artemesia Gentileschi; alive again
Suddenly, in Naples, Rome, London, Florence;
Part of the conversation. Chewed over. Proclaimed.
Dated by the metropolitan coterie; chased
By a hundred squinting critics. I find
Their euphoria, after centuries of silence, strange.
A woman has to cultivate a savage mind.
In my art Judith stands as sage.
She murders murderous Holofernes
For the liberation of her tribe, then brandishes his head -
A bleeding sign to freeze male psychopaths.
For power ousts power, often without a word
Of reason. She was my model from the start;
She is the biblical insurrection of my art.

LETTER TO THEO FROM HIS BROTHER: JUNE 1889

I am incarcerated here at St Remy.
The maniacal sun hammers the small window.
All night I think of home: the North Sea

Pounding the flat land, the dykes, drained fields,
Where razor-winds squall and blow
Gashing the geometric and metallic waters.

Yet I plan to return. For, brother, my mind
Flounders. At times I no longer know
Who or what I am; and am unable to find

A way back. Like someone sensing the water cold
Struggles to regain the bank ... I'll not go on. Theo,
Have any of my recent paintings sold

Or been talked of in Paris? It's oppressive here.
Gendarmes guard my work. The locals in the street
Turn their heads. The young kids point and stare

Coldly. I shall not now become what I might have been.
Please send more paint, all colours: cobalt,
Ultramarine, zinc, white, emerald green -

I'll daub against the darkness and in a trance
Render the sun. Cracked with voltages of blue
The plane trees rise into a yellow turbulence.

Weird forces break over me in waves.
I'll load the brush. And keep it true.
Artists are the broken vessels of their age.

EGON SCHIELE IN PRISON: APRIL 1912

*On 13th April 1912 the young painter Egon Schiele was suddenly
without explanation put into prison at Neulenbach.*

To hell with chiaroscuro! And what use
A thousand Grecian plaster casts when
My skin erupts with boils
And simmers at sexual boiling point?
Judge Savanorola there was bound to be
Misunderstanding between us. Even

When I was small you lumbered in
To burn my steam train sketches.
Art pollutes the hygiene of the mind
You said - or something like it;
And *Stick to academic subjects.*
My gangling limbs were strictly unclassical;

My appetite irregular. Here I gag with the stench
Of sweat, carbolic acid, excrement.
Some convict has gouged his initials
Deep into the wood. *MR April 1912.*
Six small leaves decorate a bone-like twig;
A spider dangles from its mangled web.

I am an insurrection of images desperate
For space. Incarcerated, I'm sick
For pencils. Charcoal. Brushes. Paint.
I jam my fingers in my mouth and scrawl
The stations of the cross in phlegm and spit.
They stay ten seconds. Then evaporate.

THE LONELINESS OF EDWARD HOPPER

*The beginning and end of all literary activity is the reproduction of
the world that surrounds me by means of the world that is within
me.*

> A quotation from Goethe carried in the artist's wallet.

Great art, you once wrote, *is the outer expression*
Of *inner life*. Your work, then, is confession
To a deeper self. Your Testimony. Your metaphor.

New York looms in yellow and black.
Stranded in a hotel somewhere, someone stares back,
Caught unaware, paralysed between the acts;

Downtown a stripper whirling her blue veil enters
Her final arc of loneliness. The white jesters
Are too far off for us to grasp their words;

Shorn of quips and puns they mime a tragic pair.
And where are you in all of this? It's all metaphor,
But I see you most clearly in the tramp steamer

Of 1908 dangerously submerged yet steaming out
Into ice-cold water. Or, again, I sense the artist
In that cliff face of 1915, gaunt and arrogant -

Ready to take whatever the day's incoming errant
Tide may bring thrashing and broiling at your feet.
And somewhere, nearby, I hear the sea divide.

It surges over the shingle bank, to sob
In seaweed in the dripping dark. Unseen.
Almost ungrasped. Paint substantiates the loss.

I chose my life. And this is how it was.

4

THE POET SPEAKS

PROLOGUE

This is not a text.
These words are not signs.
It does not concern race. Class. Gender.

This is not a silence on the page
Nor the latest Rorschach test
To prompt infantile rage or childhood trauma.

This is not a poem for contending critics.
Is not for the small margins of newspapers.
Is not a cultural resource. Not an entertainment. Not a learning aid.

This is a dispossessed cry which longs to know itself.
It starts. It stops. It hesitates.
It aches to grasp

Its shape, to own the promise of its anguish.
If it has a secret it would like accompaniment.
Hand-clap. Drum.

It breaks from the throat.
It tears the tongue. Is blood. Is scream. Is sound. Is word.
Is almost musical.

SONG OF ORPHEUS

I was the first in an unforgettable line.
Honoured. Then maligned. Inventor of the lyre.
Who failed Eurydice. Who raided the archives

Of the body. Found sex. Found death. Who from guilt
Made beauty. A lyric on the blood-soaked tongue.
Tested by fire, cleansed by water, absolved by it.

Who plucking the taut gut
Drew gulls. Drew rocks. Drew stones. Drew trees
Lumbering to the one bright edge. Who stalked

The labyrinth of bone. Who staggered through the hall
Of skulls. Who came back. Little to show:
Stark line, staccato sound, a broken cadence.

Who outsang the sirens,
Copywriters, entertainers, impresarios of a jaded time.
Whose one law is transformation.

Whose one rule is song. Who floats bleeding battered
On the tidal stream. A singing head
To calm the dizzy stars. Slow their cooling.

SONNET TO ORPHEUS

A version from Rilke.

Raise no commemorative stone. Roses
Shall blossom all summer for his sake.
For this is Orpheus. His metamorphoses
Are magical. And constant. It's fatuous to rake
The world for reasons. Once and for all,
Where there's singing there's Orpheus. His words
Are transformative as music. His oracular call
Outlasts the plastic wreaths and slogans.
It's hard for us to grasp transcendence.
For even Orpheus dreads that wrenching moment,
When he travels swiftly beyond us.
Yet when his hand slips from the lyre
There's no subterfuge. And nothing's superfluous.
Angelic imagination vaults to its freedom.

DANTE TO VIRGIL AT THE ENTRANCE TO HELL

(After Canto III of the Inferno)

David Cook: *And what about Humanity?*
Alan Clark: *I'm not concerned with abstractions of that kind*
12th November 1992 BBC 4

And so we came to that place unrecorded in books
Or maps; not found in archives or libraries.
The night smouldered without stars. At times
It was so dark I could see nothing. On all sides
There rose gagged screams, muffled sighs:
A mixture of filth, insinuation, jargon, lies.
Be economical with the truth, one says. Another cries
Humanity? What is that? Tears pricked my eyes.
And all the time a blizzard scoured the place;
A million grains of sand blistered my face.
Master, I said, *For Christ's sake who are these men?*
The answer came at once. *They are the nation's scum,*
Which rises quickly. They are maggots that worm
Their way through venison. Survivors, to the end;
Who learning the art of words become the masters of deceit;
Yet are always silent when it serves them well.
Observe them closely. For we are at the entrance into hell.
It was then I saw that banner whipping the wind,
Zig-zagging as it swirled, now *Left,* now *Right,*
Now *Low,* now *High.* Such a mob followed on -
Who would have thought Death had undone so many?
From their blotched faces blood streamed to the ground
Where bloated worms rose up, to gulp it down.

EMILY DICKINSON

She came to me with two day lilies and said:
'These are my introduction'

Dear stranger - take this lily –
It has the aroma
Of sex-
And death -

And a formality
Few plants possess -
Its green stem
Is virginity -

Its white flower
Consciousness
Stranger -
Honour its singularity -

Do not sell my witness
In the market place –
Permit no barter –
But set it - rather -

In a blue vase -
In a disused chapel -
On a distant hill -
Under the violent stars -

D.H. LAWRENCE'S FIRST LESSON: THE APPLE

Let the apple be X: The Elements of Algebra Book I

Dear student, you have my permission.
Create a revolution, if you must,
But only for the fun of it; not for social class,

Nor cash. And, whatever you do,
Continue to resist the text.
Do not let the apple be X.

Now clear away your books.
As I place this apple on your desk
Look at its freckled skin;

Observe its mellow creases, its curving lines.
See with your own clear eyes
The beauty of its blemishes.

Now touch its gloss and sheen.
Next taste the flesh, sense Autumn on your tongue,
The sourness vying with the sweetness:

A long white second of communion.
This is what you know, and this is best.
This is the Alpha and the Omega -

Before the little X.

5

OF LOVE AND SEXUALITY

THE SERPENT

*You shall lose your legs and writhe upon your belly for ever eating
dust.*

Genesis Ch. 3 v.14.

Because it was low and of the earth
It was reviled. Because it crawled
Black and sinuous, it was called
Bestial. Dirt. Filth. Slime.

Men made it curve lascivious
Round the staff of their prohibitions.
And Yahweh said *Stamp this thing down
Till the end of time. For I am a jealous*

God. Illustrious, the exterminators
Came smiling through History,
A serpent dead at their feet
Or sagging from their arms.

From the bodies of beautiful girls
They claimed to lure it, to clasp it
In iron tongs, to systematically burn it.
For the projections were rife. A serpent is

Rapacity, they said, *Lust. Appetite.*
It could gobble the sun
And keep it down. It was the succubus
That went sucking at night

Replete with guile. They named it *Satan
Samael, Lilith.* To Delphos beautiful Apollo
Came. With a *Know Thyself* and *Nothing
In Excess* he sliced off the python's head

And set up shrine. Zeus clapped hands,

Had a serpent trawled through the clouds
In his sky bird's talons. And so it was
For two thousand patriarchal years

Until oil-wells gushed with flame,
Until the tide came darkly in,
A chemical inferno,
Under a vacant sky. Now time

Spirals back to cave and wilderness.
Among snapped stalks, dead grass
It moves again. Sloughs off the old millennium.
It rises, reclaims ravaged earth. Goddess.

SAPPHO'S POEM

The opening stanza is part of a poem by Sappho; the rest has been lost.

You came and I was craving you
My wits were kindled with desire
And you set them aflame.

So let me tell you how
In your long absence I chanted your name,
A mooning adolescent,

A spell on my lips. Sometimes
I would wake deranged,
Expecting to find your hair

In my fists. And falling asleep
I would sense your quick tongue
Enter my lips. Sometimes half-crazed

I would shout your stark affirmations;
They made me divine.
I uttered them often. And in your absence

Placed quivering sanctuary lamps
Where the tide's spray cooled our limbs,
Where the rocks gave holds for our finger-tips

Marking the spot for Aphrodite. The violence
Of your visits still distracts me. *Send word.*
If you come, bring only wine.

SAPPHO'S BODY

For the soul was feathered once
Plato in the *Phaedrus*

It begins again -
Though it is as old as Plato,

As ancient as Sappho.
To imagine it, imagine

After death by fire or burning ice
Some other form of life,

An arching radiance above the sea.
Did she always exist?

Or did he dream her? Who can say?
For who can separate

What's indivisible and divide the dreamer
From the dream?

And now she's gone,
He sees her everywhere: on the up escalator,

At level four, at Tesco's, at Spar;
Sappho on the motorway,

Cruising down the fast lane
At eighty miles an hour.

For the *World News* he plays a Mozart aria;
For the *Weather Forecast*, Elgar;

For light reading the *Phaedrus*
Where it claims *the soul*

Was feathered once. Today he almost believes it.
For he can feel the ravaged wings stir

Under the integument of skin and
He remembers her.

ODYSSEUS TO CALYPSO OR THE END OF THE AFFAIR

I welcomed him with open arms; I tended him. I even hoped to give him immortality and ageless youth. But now, goodbye to him.

The Odyssey.

After the burning of the walled city I came
Wanting love of a kind, distraction, sex.
The body's healing. Satiated, I am restless again.
Sand trickles through my captive's hands;
Its dampness chills my flesh. My life abbreviates.
It sputters on dissolving wax. A sudden
Wind might snuff it out. After nine years
Of carnage there's one more journey to he made.
The encompassing blue turns slowly black;
Ghosts saunter across the bay. The past
Streams back; frail familiar voices fill my brain.
The breeze turns cool. I can no longer return
Your lover's gaze. Put on your crumpled dress.
Winter draws in with intermittent rain.

CATULLUS TO HIS MODERN LESBIA

Two a.m. So brandy brings
No more relief than tranquilisers -
The theatre in my brain is rank
With its own displays. At each swig
Of the burning stuff it grows more shameless.
Believe me Lesbia, I didn't come here

To view these things, back-street dreams, jealousy's
Sensational reels. Restless
For hours I tried to keep the lascivious
Players out. So I have become
The most reluctant voyeur
Of myself. Lesbia, I had no desire to watch

That new toy-boy of yours arch over you
Or see your taunting mouth open up
To his. There is no greater torture
For a man than this. I tell you now
I could knife him as he mounts
And suffer no remorse.

Yet tomorrow when we meet in town
What will we do? We'll smile
With automatic charm. Homo sapiens, I'll trade
In Greek philosophy and be more enlightened
Than any man on earth. We'll parade
Our licence like powdered dolls.

Let those who build high moral cages
Live in them. All those
Who judge have failed to love
Their demons well enough or failed
To find their hidden dreams - or
So I'll say. Yet when you've gone -

Anguish will start again. My jealousy
Has power to split the atom.
Indifferent to consequences, I could start
A holocaust for you. Lesbia - you lovely bitch -
Love isn't free; the licence
We proclaim will be the death of me.

MEDUSA OR A SHORT HISTORY OF SEXUALITY IN TWO AND A HALF STANZAS

Medusa was the Queen of the Gorgons, her hair was of snakes and the look of her eyes turned men to stone.

In the beginning Medusa:
She crouches at the apex,
All power is hers.
Snakes copulate round her waist,
Twist through her hair.
She swallows men like plums
And spits out the stones.
No care;
No compassion here.
Her tongue lolls out.
Her eyes stare.

Enter Perseus
With a will of his own.
Armed with a knife
He severs her lascivious head
At a single blow.
He loves what it brings.
The sweet wine of power
Pumps through his veins.
No remorse,
He stamps his black boot
On the petrified face of things.

Play back;
Start again.

THE LOVE SONG OF PETER ABELARD

When inspiration did come to me it was for writing love-songs, not the secrets of philosophy.

I want the conjunction of your looks,
Not the declension of nouns in monastic cribs;
I want the time back I mangled on books.

I want your laughter to explode in my ears;
I want the babble of your monosyllabic words;
I want your eyes moist with their singular tears.

I want the advanced theology of your finger tips,
The gravitas of your breasts against my ribs;
I want your wisdom to slide under my lips.

I want that dark delta where rivers congregate,
Where lunar tides rock in and out;
Where the flat sea, like spilt silver, stretches out.

STANLEY SPENCER'S BEATITUDE

Each new fold in her skin appearing as her age increased was a new joy to him.

Stanley Spencer in his journal.

Half a century now, they've loved like this:
Violent. Urgent. Gentle. Shy.
He's come to her insatiably, more times
Than he can count, record or possibly
Remember. And now he watches her undress;
Once more, worships the whiteness of her flesh,
Straps and stays, eyes and hooks which press
Into her sagging skin leaving those pinkish
Stipples he desires to kiss, aching to have
Her grey hair between his wrinkled finger tips.
Old age has made their lust articulate.
I love your stuff inside me, she quietly says.
Wild, crumpled flowers, their faces touch and press.
And *yes,* he says. And *yes.* And *yes.* And *yes.*

PERSEPHONE ON THE LINE

Immediately the springs of fertility ran dry and the hand of death touched mankind.

The phone rings. Then rings off.
Then rings again.
It rings most days and sometimes late
Into the night.

Some woman's playing a game
I can't make out.
Whenever I take the call I sense
Winter's there and ice.

And ice. And ice. Not a breath
Of warm life.
Then came the flow of letters;
They arrived most days -

On the faded envelope small,
Black, indelible
Was scrawled my name. Yet when I tore
It open there was

Nothing inside; nothing but
The negation
Of hope. Tonight there's a mist
On the cooling air;

Autumn's decaying leaves taste black
In my mouth.
Something that can't be spoken of
Is anxious to speak out.

As I try to sleep a shadow
Takes my place.

A child kept up beyond his years waits for
The guest to arrive;

He struggles to keep awake, but darkness
Draws down the lids
Of his eyes. And with long black fingers
Strokes his face.

6

OF DEPRESSION, ESTRANGEMENT AND DEATH

FABLE

You wake one morning and know
This is no longer your room; no longer your home.

You look in the mirror. The dread comes back.
There is a cold sweat on your forehead;

A hand-grenade sticks in your throat.
You open the cupboard; three corpses fall out.

There are no gaps for spiders or germs.
The carpet runs clean to the skirting boards.

The basement has been sealed off for years.
Nothing goes down. Nothing returns.

The clock on the mantelpiece murders history.
You open the door and God the Father stands there,

A quizzical ghost, he has nothing to say.
This is the quandary, this is the conundrum,

You will have to tackle one day.
Panic begins here. Your childhood is over.

THE MESSIAH

We had been waiting ever since we were born,
Crouched in the kitchen, where the ceiling flaked,
Or in the parlour with the curtains drawn -

As if home was the birth-place for a dread
That defied naming. The monologue of fear
Was in our eyes. Little was ever said.

Then as Spring was about to break each year,
A tall man arrived with a chalice of ash.
Thou art dust, he chanted in my ear,

And unto dust thou shalt return. With his thumb
He pressed the crumbling mark of Christ
Into our baffled flesh. My mind went numb.

We spent our lives with our knees on marble
In obscure corners with confessional voices.
Heard just out of reach. Yet I was more than sure

We would be notified when the event came,
Receive an official letter giving a date
And a place, a number and a name.

Yet he arrived unannounced. A knock on the door
On another uneventful day and the Messiah
Stood there, smooth-shaved and assured.

We nodded. And assembled like children.
He told us to leave things as they were:
The kettle steamed into the air,

The dogs yelped and scratched at the door.
We lined up like cherubim.
It was the end we had been waiting for.

ISAAC SPEAKS

And they came to the place which God had told him of; and
Abraham built an altar there, and laid the wood in order, and
bound Isaac his son, and laid him on the altar upon the wood. And
Abraham stretched forth his hand, and took the knife to slay his son.
                                                    Genesis Ch. 22 v.9-IO.

You keep dragging me down the same track -
I'd rather not -
I don't want to talk about it
It's a cul-de-sac -

Anyway, as I've said so many times before -
The symptoms are not severe -
There's just this pain in the back of my neck -
It hurts like fire -

And then there's this extreme flashing of light
Before my eyes -
A nightmare which keeps coming back - it's nothing much -
Doctor I'm alright -

You've got others in greater need at the door -
I'll sign off -
And get out of your hair - the symptoms don't last -
I'm quite sure

There's no point in going on like this - I'll shut up -
Except to say -
That the official report laid out on your desk
Is a bit of hype

For patriarchs - I don't want to talk about it - but look -
I want to know -
Who tells the stories while we go dumb and unseen -
Who writes the book

The people read? I went blind into my own story -
I carried those sticks
On my own back and kept asking Father *Why? Why?* -
But who asked me? -

I know - I know - you'll say that God's merciful angel came -
Well all I can say is -
Nice for Abraham - for me it was far too late -
Every day I wake

With my limbs knotted in ropes - shouting for life -
And see through the flames
My father's white beard and his eyes - like streaks of ice -
And catch his knife -

Doctor - I'm sorry - put it on your file marked paranoia
If you like -
My hour is up - another Isaac's knocking at the door -
I'd better go.

THE NIGHTMARE

Each night it recurs. The sublime
Jolts into nightmare. In my dream -
Gangrenous, encrusted, floating green -
God's severed head floats on the sea:
Long submerged and suddenly set free.
The ocean's frowning avatar,
Sun-drenched.

Then words gush from its stammering mouth –
Their broken sense
Drowned in the tidal turbulence;
And I who would he its witness
Wake to sweating darkness.
Psychotic five a.m.
Alarm clock ticking like a bomb.

THIS HEAD

I woke with this marble head in my hands

George Seferis

Between my hands this ancient head, unclaimed.
I picked it up in a shocking dream
And could not put it down again. Half-crazed
Curator, I want it to be seen.

Its eyes stare into a radiance beyond our grasp;
Its face peels with burning skin.
Though it may desire to speak to us,
A fastidious mouth shuts it in.

I will ransack archives, break gummed seals,
Crack open vaults, desecrate graves
To find its world and speak for him.
Two lives are over. A third begins.

THE MELANCHOLIC SPEAKS

Do you remember Durer's *Melancholia,* how
She sits inconsolable?
How her carved wings weigh down like lead;
How with no angelic movement left
A bent arm resolutely buttresses
A slumping head?

That is how it feels most days.
I testify.
And do you recall how at her feet
Lie the assorted instruments of work: pincers,
Knife, nails, plane - all discarded
As if nothing she had made could ever meet

Or satisfy the first
Inordinate intentions of the heart?
And the hour-glass and the bell
Tell that time is passing
And has passed; and *now* is far too late
To start again. Behind her (well

Out of reach) stand the ladder
And the magic square. Did those numbers
Fail to correlate
And that tall ladder step
Into appalling space? Despair
Enters immovable as fate.

How could this stone seraphim
Ever soar again
Into the glory of angelic life?
Even her companion dog slumps
A carcase at her feet
And the apocalyptic light

Above the sea is sham
Like manufactured tinsel. Today
I feel I was born
Into this place, where angels petrify.
And sleep when it comes comes dreamless.
Death's automaton.

THE DEATH OF RAINER MARIA RILKE 29TH DECEMBER 1926

Rose, oh the pure contradiction, delight of being no one's sleep under so many lids.

Rilke's own epitaph.

His enchanted life moves to disenchantment again:
I am an empty space. Have never been.
Now nothing helps towards myself. Life can
Slacken in mid-sentence; crack at a hyphen.
First the child and then the man step past,
Only to blur, to be utterly cancelled.
No face comes back from the transparent glass;
The lake regains its ancient solitude.
You have feared annihilation like this since
A child drowning in your father's eyes.
It flutters in like anaesthetising snow. Angelic
Death has come an overwhelming distance
At such slow speed to bring this end:
This Flower Huge White Inconceivable And -

THE COLD HOUR OF VIRGINIA WOOLF

(All italicised passages in this poem have been taken in no particular order from the late journal entries of Virginia Woolf.)

In the cold hour
This
Before the lights go up

Low tide
Flat water on the flat sand

Yet I was thinking we live without a future
That's what's queer
With our noses pressed to a closed door

On the other side it advances inch by inch
Over the crumbled jigsaw of stone mud sand shell bone
The sky breaks a flint dawn

A week of broken water impends
We pour to the edge
Of the precipice
And then

It arrives crosshatched by wind all motion
Slaps the wharf's wood engulfs foundations
Folds the river's estuary back upon itself

I walk over the marsh saying
I am I
And must follow that furrow
Not copy another

Cold and sinuous among reed and detritus
It fills the bed gurgles in gullies

Licks wet the dry cracks
Blindly rhapsodic
The distant sun laying it into gold

And want nothing
But sleep
Infinitely lit and tinted
And cold and soft

Brimming the flood-banks it comes
To its climax *Oh may the flood last*
For ever As it was in the beginning
Then a swoon a drain and then
Slackens recedes as much as it came
Dragged back by the lunar tide
It empties out

Terrifying
I suppose so

In the cold hour
Before the lights go up

I THINK THEREFORE IBM

What's the use of what is Good?
Put Beauty out to fashion. As for Philosophy
Go for the copy. I think therefore etcetera.

Mozart's body, vehicle for the great sublime,
Lies in a pauper's hole, sprinkled with lime;

Van Gogh prowls among the confined insane –
The sunflower petals are blades in his brain;

Slumped in a wheelchair Nietzsche dribbles and dozes:
Dionysius crucified. An experiment closes.

Susanne Langer discards her *Opus* on mind –
Her great enlightenment goes by degrees blind.

What's the use of what is Good?
There's no future in Tragedy. I think
Therefore. Etcetera, etcetera, etcetera.

FALLEN MAN WITH ONE WING

Only the youngest brother, whose sleeve she had had no time to finish, had a swan's wing instead of an arm...

From the Grimms' *The Six Swans*

Please don't ask who I am. I'm a stranger here.
Have no parents. No clear past. No fixed address.
I am a catalogue of questions with only riddles
For answers. I limp boundaries, stumble through war-zones
Where history meanders, breaks off, locks on itself.
I struggle each day to keep two feet on the ground.
Death sticks in the palm of my hand like a hand-grenade.

From where did I fall? From what height to what depth?
What time was it then? Was it night? Were there stars
In the vault of the sky? Or was it the heart of day?
Were there strips of blue out over the sea?
Was anyone there? Did they record my fall?
All the bureaucratic forms, all the files are blank.
Then, who spun the garment which half covers my skin?
Who draped it over my head? It nettles and stings.

Amnesiac under the sun, the more I question
The less I understand. And what is this wing where
An arm should be? This shaming thing. This dark
Impediment. And who put a star on my brutish brow
To mark me out for what inscrutable purpose?
It burns. I touch it. There's gold on my hand.
I'm on trial here. Much of the time I'm out
Of my mind. I scrawl notes when I can.

It is evening. The sun falls through amber.
We could be near the end of Winter.

7

OF TRANSFORMATION AND RENEWAL

THE HEALING OF PHILOCTETES

I am of dubious gender, of split mind.
The epileptic at the door. The abused child.
The criminal hammered into wood.

Loneliness predates my birth.

I was once the unspeakable sadness of God,
The gash in his plenitude, the shadow in his thought,
The hole in his heart. When his experiment faltered

I was his first tear.

And during that interminable Greek war
I was the one abandoned at Lemnos,
A suppurating wound in my foot. A running sore,

It stank worse than excrement.

It appalled the nostrils of the world.
Here I mastered the art of the bow, until life
Sang in the string.

Now the running stag shudders. And falls.

Now each arrow, released, splices the wood
Or splits the skin to pierce the bone,
Entering the blood stream forever.

A kestrel drops from the sky like stone.

Each shot as exact as it is ultimate.
At my stricken foot the quarry mounts.
Slowly, I mend.

I scan horizons.

I see Paris dead, the ten year carnage over.
There's Ulysses en route to Ithaca.
I see Aeneas set out for Crete, Carthage, Rome.

Flesh seals the wound. History storms on.

OPHELIA'S KNOWLEDGE

After Odilon Redon's painting *Ophelia Among the Flowers*

Ophelia knows more than Hamlet knows
Though the skull lies between the fingers of his questions.

Far out from the royal court Ophelia floats
Her body tangled in dream's dredge-nets;

Her face becomes a sacred mask through whose
Gaping mouth the salt truth spumes and flows.

Her eyes open into darkness where flowers –
Blue-black blue-green blue-white - silently explode.

Such beauty in endarkenment! Yet between grave-stones
Hamlet struts. Mutters. Soliloquises. Questions questions.

THE HOUSE OF IMAGINATION

After Rilke

Is it possible
that throughout recorded time we have merely tripped through a
maze
reflecting ourselves over and over and over again,
sleepwalkers in caves, overlooking the fact that all mazes have
entrances
and therefore exits?
It is possible.

Is it possible
that until now our hands have only stretched over the surface of
things,
not sensing their silent interiors,
their monastic centres?
It is possible.

Is it possible
that we have yet to phrase those questions of ultimate simplicity,
that we have still to grasp the hopes which razor our hearts,
that there are a myriad of reasons not yet announced?
It is possible.

Is it possible
that we have allowed words like Freedom, God, History to become
so monumental
that they have eclipsed our more intimate tasks,
our everyday actions such as peeling an apple,
talking to a friend
or simply staring out of the window?
It is possible.

Is it possible
that we have still to begin, to set out,

still to pluck the stars from the firmament
and place them in the bowl of our mind;
and that, after aeons of time, the stars are still waiting for us
to create this superlative lustre?
It is possible.

It could be.

IN DEFENCE OF THE RAVEN

And it came to pass at the end of forty days that Noah opened the window of the ark which he had made: and he sent forth a raven, which went forth to and fro, until the waters were dried up from off the earth. Also he sent forth a dove.

Genesis Ch. 8 v. 6-8

It did not leave at once. For two hours
Or more it perched on the ark,
Eyeing the waves and the slanting horizon:
A dark witness under storm clouds.

Nor, when it finally left, did it go lightly.
At first, unsure of direction, it flew
Without grace. An equivocation of wings,
A mere inch above drowning water.

By all means cherish the dove. It returned
Loyally with good news in its beak.
So make it your icon on banners of peace
And hang them over the warring cities.

But, at night, as you try to sleep, remember
Far horizons, black holes, exploded nova stars;
Remember the curved edge of God's
Incommensurable mind – where the raven flies.

8

CODA

NEW CONSTELLATIONS

One often hears: that is good but it belongs to yesterday. But I say:
yesterday has not yet been born. It has not really existed. I want Ovid,
Pushkin and Catullus to live once more.
Osip Mandelstam.

You do not begin alone; rather, you extend
A narrative. Through the half-open window
The breeze blows in spiked with salt
And distance. Your senses stir until
Your memories rise into new constellations.
Who said that there can be no more beauty? That art
Must be minimal or brutal: an ideological aid
Or bare reflection – a mirror laid across
A gallery floor. Or some such dull cleverness?
The mind's traffic jams in the maze of the sign,
Ironic civilisation silts and chokes itself.
These words lie dark on the field of the page:
Hard, obdurate grains against the age.

The past, which never truly was, returns again.

from

ANGELIC IMAGINATION

1997

THE WORD

In the beginning was the wound.
It bled. Perpetual haemorrhage.
So huge it longed to close itself; so raw
It wanted death.
There was no end to it.
Blood filled the void to vein the world.
It entered time to stain each second.
And from the wound came the word
So extreme it was beautiful;
So pure it was absolute. It demanded
An answer. It went in quest.
A swift of interrogation
It flew through the hole of pain.
It needed to know.
Its flight was remorseless.
After aeons of time
It returned with its poem:
Blood could bear more than itself.
It could mother us.
It could father us.
Dark and unknown.
The wound was but the beginning.

And now the bird waits
Quivering for its next flight,
Next quest, next poem.

POSSESSION

After Sappho

- just like a god - that man -
who sits over there -
all eyes - all ears -
falling for your every word -

when I glance at both of you -
fire gashes my neck -
sweat oozes from my hair -
the words jam -

my tongue is splintered glass -
I see only blackness -
in my drumming ears
Syracuse crashes -

I am white ash
at the boundaries of death –
motes of dust
in the lashing gale -

I am as free
as the moth driven
into the scorching wick –
into the burning flame -

MARRIAGE SONG

To Annabel and Matthew on their Wedding.

1

Came Idaeus...
Messenger...
Swift...
With immortal fire...
And Hector....
With his dark-eyed girl...
Over the sea...
Bracelets and trinkets...
Gold silver...
They were like gods...
And music from the flute...
And lyre...

2

Everywhere...
Scattered...
Under the olive tree...
Bowls....
Chalices...
Aroma of myrrh...
Incense...
Women shouting...
Men singing...
Then...
The green distillation of the harp...
For Hector...
And Andromache...

SUDDEN LOVE

After Sappho

And love bludgeoned my senses -
A gale across the mountain slopes -
Wrenching out the ancient oaks.

PETER ABELARD'S CALAMITY IN 1118

There was in Paris at the time a young girl named Heloise
Historia Calamitatum

Love drew our eyes together
 far more than
the lesson to the page.

Out of his crimson dream
prodigal
she steps again:

Heloise. They gaze at each other
before the start of time;
into his ravenous mouth

her tongue slips,
sweet as honey,
wise as wine.

This is the cave of metaphor.
This is the portal
of song.

Galaxies explode. Civilizations blossom
and age. A small fly
settles on the unread page.

A TEMPEST FOR OUR TIMES

Ariel is no longer here. Her spirit
Dissolved into thin air, the vaguest kind
Of memory now. Did she ever flit
Through our intactable world for love of mind?
But Caliban's back! He's come up triumphant,
A disc-jockey in a silk suit, pimp
Of the mega-machine. He grunts at us
In monosyllables and grins at his luck.
And Prospero? Senex and Mage he sits
Through this interminable committee-meeting,
Stats and facts at ten finger-tips:
To report back *in due course when etcetera.*

Lights to dim until it is so dark
The absence of light in dark can be discerned.

ON SEEING VERMEER'S KITCHEN-MAID IN THE RIJKSMUSEUM

For Miranda

It arrests you as you stroll until you reel,
Almost breathless, dizzy with the thing seen.

Monumental in dark blues and yellows –
The maid stands steadying a household jug.

The white milk flows from vessel to vessel.
World thickens. Time bulks. Breath slows.

Crowds pass - cameras snap - guides give their spiel.
But you must stand here alone, seeing and unseen.

On the table before her, unbroken loaves;
Behind her ineffable light floods in.

EDVARD MUNCH: SELF-PORTRAIT WITH A CIGARETTE

Disease and madness and death were the black angels standing over my cradle.

I

From out of the dark I appear
Tomorrow's ghost,
Wreathed in blue
And claustrophobic smoke:
A Lutheran assailed by doubt,
Calvin without his Christ -
Leaning back
And staring out.
I wait to ambush Being
Make it speak
Her native language:
Her black and crimson speech.

II

When I was born three angels fell
From a snow-dead sky -
Their wings were black,
Eyes blind.
I paint to bring my mother back.
I wrap her in cool lilac,
Wheel her into a Northern sky
Under a chromatic sun.
She died
When I was five.

III

At fifteen my sister died.
Tired Orpheus of the Underworld

I've been down to fetch her
Fifty times!

With her flowing auburn hair
She rises: *The Sick Child.*

Terror trained my finger tips;
Death schooled my mind.

Look at her convalescent face;
She never died.

An ice-wind blows
Across infinite space.

IV

I fight three angels -
In my dreams.

With their feathers
I daub these marks,

With our blood
I make this frieze.

Earth shivers.
Sky bleeds.

FRIEDRICH NIETZSCHE AROUND 1889

As if he came from a place where no one else lives

Edwin Rohde

I scrawl my metaphors in the dust –
I cannot see life steadily
Nor can I see it whole –
The candle flares on dwindling wax.

The wind's calligraphy on the sea
Makes random marks
Dissembling meaning.
I cannot play my hand, nor let it pass.

Life's plenitude streams the other side of glass.
I would affirm. Spent stars
Gash the midnight air.
Here comes a candle to light you to bed -

Here comes a chopper to chop off your head.
More light - more dark.
I have tried to affirm life -
But ah!

THE SHADOW ON BONNARD'S FACE

Hard on himself, haunted, self-effacing,
He stoops before us, reticent. And questioning.
A shadow darkens the length of his face.
Can this be Bonnard who affirms our place
As modern alchemists and brought Paradise
To the Villa du Bosquet? Painting after painting
Where seeing is sacramental and metaphysics
Carnal as wine, as red as apples ripening
On a white cloth, blue as the sea's distance.
And Martha sets his imagination free.
Hour after hour she baths for him - God's
Voyeur! Even the dead tiles change their hues;
Resurrect in greens, yellows, ochres, blues -
A surplus for the goddess as the water cools.
And then this shadow darkening across his face.

ARTIST'S MANIFESTO

For Lynne Gibson

The artist detonates his mind to let in God's.
Under his loaded brush the world ignites.

Perception burns to vision. Metaphysics
Dance in his eyes. Under his finger-tips

All life's transmutation, an alchemist's laboratory
For experiments. Oh! - to set the imagination free

In the hard crucible of nature, to begin
To murder fate, to let the incandescent angel in!

WITTGENSTEIN IN CAMBRIDGE

There are, indeed, things that cannot be put into words. They make
themselves manifest. They are what is mystic.

Tractatus Logico-Philosophicus.

After the austerity of the Cambridge-seminar
He dives into the local cinema;

The kids climb the seats, wolf-whistle and flirt;
The side-lights dim. The great beneficent dark

Streams over his tousled head. The magical actors
Rise on the screen. This is the academy of dreams.

Here desire manifests itself; here life begins.
Ah, no more seminars! No more syllogisms!

THE LEOPARD

After Rilke

The leopard sidles the length of its cage.
Bars. And more bars. Again and again
To be arrested by iron. Its eyes glaze.
A fatwa of iron is stamped on its brain.

The fierce trajectory of its stride slows
To a circular crawl. No life can enter.
Only its paws now track the burning forest.
A ring of fire. An exploded centre.

PSALM

After Paul Celan

No-one can create us again out of the dust
No-one.

Never.

Hallowed be thy name, No-one.
Who is not in heaven.

Not the Power.

Nor the Glory.

For your sake
We live and flower.

We are not roses -
Our stamens broken,
Our stems blood red.

Not in the beginning.

Nor in the end.

Flowering now and for never.
Without

Amen.

ANGELIC IMAGINATION

A Poem in Five Movements
In Memory of Kate Cooper: Young Composer

1

Child, your blonde locks gone,
    bald-headed,
        involuntary Buddha
you walk among us
    prematurely wise. Your nine
        brief years
make our more casual time
    seem mean
        and almost criminal.
On an unseen boundary line
    you hover and dance,
        a recorder at your lips;
Allegro and *Andante* arch
    absurdly beautiful above
        the savagery of chance.
Stranded in safer places we are
    your sad and
        feckless witnesses
as now you fight your failing lungs
    for one more
        blast of breath-
to blow a final cadence
    of beauty
        against your death.

2

Almost a spectre now, still
      whispering *yes,* wanting
          the shamanic flute
for the hesitant breath.
      At each blow life,
          brief and equivocal,
blossoms at the stem.
      Dear mortal child how
          you defy
the body's cancerous duplicity.
      From the plenitude
          of sound
an ultimate simplicity.
      So promiscuous Death
          give over!
Beyond all trauma her breath
      hurls out its
          musical hosanna.

3

Dear child, my darling Orpheus,
    you have called on Death
        and heard its pitiless *No*
and now return to play for us
    Andante and *Allegro.* Fearless,
        you walk a lonely isthmus
between rising tides,
    music at your lips, recorder
        in your hands.
Where squalling wind is deaf and
    staring ocean blind,
        your *allegro* rises up,
pierces the distraught mind.
    The music mounts
        the hostile air
and almost heals. And almost mends.
    Spirit begins
        where nature ends.

4

Who comes at noon who
     waits in doorways
         lingers in the afternoon
who stammers who smiles who
     teazes who burns deceit
         who scorches ease
who runs between the slanting rain
     who answers gulls who
         scrawls her name
under their wild white wings
     who is the lexicon of love
         the syntax of tears
who is the freight of dreams
     who disappears who
         returns with Orpheus
whose music rises as breath
     fragrant as memory
         as intangible as death

5
(After Rilke)

Raise no commemorative stone.
     Roses shall blossom
         all summer for her sake -
for she is Orpheus whose change
     of key is magical
         and constant.
Fatuous to ask nature for its reasons.
     Once and for all:
         Where there's music
She's there. Her urgent call
     transfigures
         and turns to dust
the plastic wreaths and slogans.
     It's hard for us
         to grasp transcendence.
Even Orpheus dreads that moment
     when she must move
         beyond us-
Yet when her hand slips from
     the quivering instrument
         there's no subterfuge
and nothing's superfluous.
     Angelic imagination
         vaults to its freedom.

TOO NEAR TO DEATH

You have been too near to death too long;
In the silent cancer wards watching lives,
Once beautiful and loud with hope, decay;
And now you stand alone, huge with grief

And inconsolable. So much undone.
So much you did not know. Nor do. Nor say.
Minute particles of grief lie on every book
And photograph; and on every random wind

A dry incriminating dust blows in.
At each door in every corridor
Promiscuous death stands with his letcher's grin
And life's the calamity no-one talks about.

INTIMATIONS OF MORTALITY

Late November and the first frosts are cleansing
This place. There are gaps in the trees;
Irregular holes in the fence. The neighbours
Are incinerating the leaves

And I imagine myself not here.

The flames poke through the shriveled heaps;
Last month's decapitated heads disappear
In thin meandering smoke. It drifts across
The boundary into our home

And I imagine myself not here.

Today the frosted lawn is a beautiful
Altar cloth, starched and crisp, and laid out
For no god. The pond is a sheet of glass;
It returns the sky. Immaculate. Blue. Silent. Vast.

REMEMBER THIS YOUNG MAN FOREVER YOUNG

In Memory of Paul Grant: 1974-1995

Remember this young man, forever young,
A shy smile on his young man's lips -
And among his many friends loved for
Loyalty, gentleness, his sense of life and risk.
Remember his skill and its evolving craft,
Dexterous hand cutting the frangible glass -
Composing his own *Toccata and Fugue*
In metaphysical reds and greens and blues.
His incomplete design soars above us;
Dazzles the dark, outstares the bitter loss.
We are a tower of dreams. A desert of ash.
A galaxy of stars. A handful of dust.
Once. And only once. And then no more.

Cherish this fragile life. Remember Paul.

THE NIGHT JOURNEY

For Theodore

Go down these steps but enter slowly.
The door opening cuts a rectangle of light.
A dark room. A hidden labyrinth underground.

Earth's smell clamps nose and throat;
The vaulted silence takes my breath away.
Weren't you ever told this place was out of bounds?

When the next door opens a faded, cobwebbed, light
Breaks through. An orange butterfly flits across.
Can you remember it now? Does it come back?

Slowly it returns. The aroma of honey coating the dust -
And all that bee-keeping paraphernalia:
The long white vestments, the black-meshed hoods,

Those glinting containers, those silver drums,
A liquid gold dripping from their sticky taps -
The jam-jars brim-full of the golden stuff.

Then up three steps and slowly out,
Squinting into the light of an ordinary day -
The sun dropping behind the charcoal woods.

And what does it all mean to you now? Can you say?
I imagine substances growing in the dark beneath.
Alchemical. Strange. Silent. Out of reach.

IN THE BEGINNING

In the beginning was the Word.
It became flesh.
It walked amongst us.
It stuttered its own meaning.
It was its own enigma.
It spoke in paradox.
It dreamed.

It was not comprehended.
It was cornered by questions.
It was crowned with thorns.
It was nailed to a tree.
It tasted vinegar.
It was pierced through the side.
It screamed.

It was placed in a tomb.
It came back.
It was Word again.
It uttered its distilled meanings.
It was Song.
It was free.
It redeemed.

From

LOVE AFTER SAPPHO

1999

NAVIGATING DARKNESS

Sometimes I think of us: obscure spiders
Spinning from our entrails metaphysical webs,
Acrobats who hang from a single thread

Dancing awkwardly to silk the sullen emptiness,
To weave together disparate things, leaf and ledge,
Branch and bridge, the vital and the dead.

Our fragile geometries shimmer over the abyss.
Or sometimes I see us through another image:
That athletic girl on a warm Minoan hill;

Upside down, she somersaults the charging bull –
A red speck of transcendence against the blue.
A mere child. Inviolable. Free. And falling still.

And then I think of Sappho: *the lightest breath*
Yet my words live on - in the acoustic chambers
Of our mind's navigating darkness beyond the stars.

POST-MODERN LOVE

I do not know what way to move; I am of two minds

Sappho

KAMIKASE STARS

Brutal in the heart of August winter slips in,
Strips the green foliage, burns the green leaves.
Cool on my brow. Cold on your fingers.

An oil drum flares without a sound.
Pyramids of skulls rise from the smoking ground.
A war-lord patrols his cardboard town.

Insubstantial ghost I pace the wooden floor.
What for? What ultimately for?
Our lacerating days go out like all the others.

The guru in the Book of Wisdom speaks:
Throw the dice twice - then leave it to the play of chance.
The kamikase stars blaze into the infinite.

Divided lovers, where are we?
Under the smouldering rubble. Under the burning sea.

LAS VEGAS PERHAPS

There's this city I am driving to. Las Vegas –
Perhaps. Its gaudy beads of light seduce,
Release adrenalin. I'm in a stolen car
And travelling fast. Suddenly, it blows a tyre.
The vehicle somersaults, bursts into fire.
I scramble out - my hair's ablaze - and shout –
For Christ's sake help. The traffic neither stops
Nor brakes. The drivers turn their ghostly heads –
And then accelerate... Love, there are no words
For dreams like this. They detonate the mind.
Where was I running from?
What was I running for?
This numbing loss - this age-old fear.
Tell me I still exist... Stroke my burning hair.

SPEAKING OF EROS

Gilded, you said, they were gilded by love;
It was as if when they smiled the gods above
Poured honey over them. Their limbs were gold
And shone transparent. As you spoke a cold

Sweat broke over me. I knew if I had the power
I would have had them executed in the public square,
Hung, drawn, quartered or crucified upside down,
Their honeyed limbs dragged over common ground –

And would have shredded all lies in their defence,
For ease of civilization requires a formal reticence.
Then later came those swarming flies –
Buzzing through my mouth, my ears, my socket-eyes.

A MANTRA OF ACCIDENTAL LIGHT

Time has no purpose, but you come again
To grace my life. Love's jaded jargon cries
On my tongue, bitter with past betrayals,
Ancient battles, festered scars, tabloid lies.

Love's a plastic tag on merchandise
And Eros a pornographer. Under every word
An angel bleeds, dragged from the arching sky,
And raped and blinded. Cupid, you have become

A crazed, degraded thing - a crass hard-on
For every predilection. Who now can speak of
Love's celestial influence? Today I return
Your steadfast glance without a word.

The furnace sun is bronze upon your hair.
A mantra of accidental light. A form of prayer.

AT CUCKMERE ESTUARY

We stand on the shingle as night comes in. Behind us
Storm clouds, bruised and red, slump to the Downs. This is
The last violence of the haemorrhaging sun. Lightning forks

And flickers vertical at the edge. All that our eclectic times
Have claimed dissolves. We listen to a silence whose signs
Are hard and hazardous to read. We are novices. New-comers.

Inland a siren wails and spreads its shrill alarm. At last
The stillness returns more intensely reticent for the dissonance.
The reason is... The reason is... There are no reasons left;

Platitudes jostle in the gaps. The healing word takes flight
In the daily battle-ground of microphones and hype
And singing Orpheus drowns in a flood of camera light.

We close our eyes and sense the breeze against our flesh.
The salt burns our mouths. There's no desire to talk. We drink
In the forgotten dark. The tide spumes white against the chalk.

LAST RITES

But all must be endured

Sappho

AT CROMER HOSPITAL

Mother, I sit powerless by your bed.
Crouched under newly laundered sheets,
Your body has shrunk to that of a child.
Your face is cracked, eyes blue as cornflowers.
You shouldn't have come all that way to see me,
I'm alright... A few days left to live, self-effacing
As ever. Though you can barely lift a child's
Beaker to your lips, you ask for barley water.
The drip-feed's off; there'll be no more solids.
Once, I'd have done anything for you;
A timid boy, I loved you to excess.
Outside the ward June's burning laburnum
Spills on the world a fading radiance.
The morphine zips in to ease the dying.

ALL NIGHT IN HOSPITAL

All night in hospital I hold your hand
And ache to sleep. Unread newspapers litter
Your room. Unwanted food, unwanted drink
Stand on the window sill. Here time neither ticks
Nor moves but hangs silent and oppressive.
A patient in another ward screams out - a flurry
Of movement - a metal trolley clatters down
An unseen corridor. In an urgent track of time
Someone, somewhere, is dying. Almost dawn –
Outside the senile day begins. Birds repeat
Their morning platitudes, blank clouds gather.
Grotesquely the sun breaks through. Mother,
What can we place against such huge indifference?
A hand across the skull. Love's glance. This breath.

TRAVELLING TO A FOREIGN LAND

And now flowers in their glass cases burn
With furious incandescence. Red.Yellow.
Blue. Absurdly beautiful.
I hold your frail veined hands.
Put vaseline on your lips, lavender water
On your brow. Our final ritual. You slip
Into sleep, stir, start to hallucinate.
Strange animals stalk the place. Silver spoons
Rise in the room and then, an oracle, you speak;
Feelings are hard to portray... You must understand
The other view... It's like travelling to a foreign land.
Mother, I have never heard you quite so eloquent.
I squeeze your hands and kiss your dried out lips –
As the vessel of our lives drifts to the precipice.

EXTREME UNCTION

Today the priest arrives. He holds the crucifix
For you to kiss. He makes the sign of Christ
Upon your frowning brow, your dried-out lips.
I stand awkward. I cannot kneel nor say
Amen... As a child I prayed for life eternal;
Now life dissolves under our finger-tips.
We lurch to our extinction. And die alone.
This is the poison which blisters the skin;
This is the chemical which corrodes the bone.
Holy Mary, Mother of God, pray for us
Sinners now and at the hour of our death –
At the end of taste – at the end of touch –
At the end of speech – at the end of breath –

A GIRL IN SEPIA

Mother, there's still a bitterness on my tongue
And iron rusts near my heart. It's hell
To speak the truth. With you, I seldom did.
Absurdly shy, I was the kind of child who stared
And stuttered, to find long after the event the words
He hungered for. Tonight I look through photographs;
Here you are, a girl - in sepia - your First Communion:
All curls and frills. And here you are - in black and white –
Eighteen. Young. And vulnerable. And beautiful.
And here decades later - in Kodak colour –
The small, huddled, stubborn woman I remember.
I still wince before your flawed, excessive love;
Yet now, far too late, beyond the grave –
Ache to thank you - for the life you gave.

LOVE'S LABOUR

I think that someone will remember us in another time.

Sappho

LOVE'S UNICORN

Somewhat after Rilke

It never was. It never ran through tall grass.
It never tasted ice water on its tongue.
It never felt the salt wind nipping the nape of its neck.
It never saw the whiteness of its body.
It never was. It could never be.

Then, one day, you longed for its existence.
Slowly it emerged, intangibly it came.
It moved in the shadows, hovered in the soul's undergrowth.
Its nostrils quivered, its clean eyes opened –
As if waiting for you to call its name.

And suddenly you said the secret word: *unicorn!*
A single horn broke from its stark brow.
Startlingly white. Precise. Spiralling to a point.
Ah! It existed then - in the silver mirror of your longing.
And that which never was, became.

GIRL WITH A FLUTE

I think today of Osip Mandelstam at the edge
Of his charred life, pacing the streets of Voronezh,
A scorched bird locked in an iron cage,
Small head, tilted back, screaming his rage:
I am the tree-splitting storm - rain zig-zagging the glass
The gargoyle frothing with water - Dante, Villon, Mozart –
The open mouth of God. Drawn to they know-not-what
The town kids jeer and shout: *General! General!* – but
Soon they will be mouthing his satirical songs,
His anti-Soviet doubt, his musical codas –
Each poem a mantra of defiant breath
Against the status quo, against his martyr's death.
What to think now? What cause should one salute?
A cadence in the wind. A girl with a flute.

A METAPHYSICAL SAPPHO; ON READING GILLIAN ROSE'S *LOVE'S WORK*

For David Evans

And every sentence thrown out's a baited hook
To catch the drifting intellect - to hurl it back
Into its turbulent element, but deeper down and

Further out. There's no softness in this glinting book.
We're born askew. Wounded. Inherently off-track.
All life's a mess and love's dialectical. We're bound

To fail, so let's fail well - take on the eloquence
Of plunging dolphins or hunted whales that sing
In bloody water their strange and piercing psalms:

I will stay in the revel of ideas and risk;
Learning, failing, wooing, grieving, trusting, working, reposing –
In this sin of language and lips...

Keep your mind in hell and despair not. Stand free
In the broken middle. You did. And failed us - brilliantly.

ALCHEMISTS DOWN THE AGE

This is the beginning of a poem. It is a vessel
For disparate things. Each day brings an element,
Unclassified, raw, incalcitrant. Car crash,

A burning head, glass. The lilac massing purple
At the window, a word in the discarded paper,
Stray threads of a marriage. Blood. Coriander. Ash.

Then the power's switched on. Flames lick the flask,
Blacken the base. Nothing's clear but the task;
The stirring, testing, tasting - that slow thickening

As the heat rips. What is it that I'm after?
An enduring amalgam that fuses the parts.
Was this the labour for gold? The philosopher's ring?

I think of alchemists down the age, god's poets –
Artisans working through the insomniac hours –
With burnt fingers, charred skin, cracked hands.

DESCENDANTS OF THE FIREBALL

Eros... sweet-bitter, impossible creature

Sappho

UNDER THE BURNING SYCAMORE

We walk through the autumn wood. Time is the cadence
Of our falling steps, the rhythm of our passing.
What can assuage our transience –

So briefly breath condenses in the air. Shrivelled leaves
And twigs lodge in our clothes and streaming hair.
The Buddha says *All things pass*

Work on your life with diligence. When did he say these words?
Under what forsaken tree? And when did we stroll into
The smouldering wreckage of this wood?

Memories break, fade, go slack. Chrysanthemums shed
Their dark aroma; their crowns are packed with death.
A silence beats against my head

Its chill amnesia. We are spindrift prone to dream,
Our hours cremating into ash. Under the burning sycamore
The blackbird sings our requiem.

PISCES

We draw our astrological sign on sand
As the brackish tide comes in, crass lovers,
Imagining the world as ours - as if our hand
Could map love onto the burning planets,

Black holes, imploding stars. *In the beginning*
A vast explosion. An incomparable violence.
Then who are we? And where do we fit in?
Creatures of chaos, quirks of chance.

Our astrological signs are sealed and coded songs;
They cannot disclose the purpose of the galaxies
Nor grace this barren shore. Ceaseless tongues
Of salt erase our zodiacal scrawl.

Only inside our fraying lives these marks are more.
An unbounded surplus - not maps, but metaphor.

DARK WITH SNOW

All day white flakes circle the occluded sun,
Bits of nothing the ice wind has blindly shaped.
They mount on slate and twig and window sill.
The suburb's rubbed out, the world's a shroud –

Its violence stilled. We switch on the news:
Hazardous conditions. Northern cities at a standstill.
All main-line stations closed. Most motorways.
The freezing mist obliterates the amber light;

Our window's dark with driven white.
At four o'clock it's starless night.
Under the glass the bitterness seeps in.
Love, where are we in this rage of ice,

This eschatology of fading light, this ashen glow?
Our words make frantic marks across the snow.

JEWELS OF CONSCIOUSNESS

Love, listen - we exist to surpass ourselves,
To break the boundaries of our cells, *to cancel* –
To transcend! Nothing in nature tells us
Who we are. Consider the music of the spheres –
Random blips, distant howls, inhuman blurs.
Planets collide... Huge stars explode...
Black holes devour matter... Quasars implode.
Nature's a terrorist who enters fast. She decrees
The law of entropy to every part,
Scrubs clean the archives of the brain, with no heart,
For no purpose, for no God, for no justifying art –
Blots out memory, annuls the past.
So who are we in all of this? Small, dazzling
Jewels of consciousness - against the dark.

LA VITA NUOVA

Oltre la spera che piu larga gira
passa 'l sospiro ch'esce del mio core:
intelligenza nova, che l'Amore
piangendo mette in lui, pur su lo tira.

Beyond the sphere turning with widest gyre
Out of my heart a sign ascends:
A new intelligence that weeping love
Bestows attracts him ever higher.

Dante

THE NAMING OF THINGS

Intimate stranger, I name for you what things I can –
Demotic daisy, prophetic dandelion,

Jasmine, freesias, acanthus, saxifrage,
A litany of scattered names,

Plucked from the hurricane of riven time,
Syllables to set against oblivion –

Their cadence rides our urgent breath
Flowering before the void of death –

Yet who can restore, what can atone
The melanoma of skin, the necrosis of bone,

Mind's alzheimers, cancer of doubt,
Sudden unmeaning, slackening, the blackening out?

Bewildered naming in the thick of time:
Demotic daisy. Prophetic dandelion.

ON A JOURNEY

On a journey I read of a future in which rancour
Played no part, where no trauma
Lifted the compulsive finger to pluck again the canker

Of the past and as I looked out of the window
I watched the Downs with their flow
Of dips and curves and it was as though what I saw

Was no more than the crystallizing dream of what I'd read:
Life choreographed to time. A horse cantered
In the wind. A gate opened into clouds. A crow blacked

Over my head. A white path zig-zagged into the unknown.
And listen, each thing said. *Nothing
Is ever the same again. Observe. Integrate. Transcend.*

THE AURA OF YOUR FACE

Who can describe the aura of your face?
A proof of the existence of God? Perhaps.
Today the sun's vertical light descends as grace

Through towering clouds to enlighten our late
Estrangement and I recall those Chinese paintings,
Long landscape scrolls, where in the firmament

Through rising scrawls of mist a small tree
Hangs over the abyss to blossom there - suddenly
White, frail, incomparable. *Imago dei.*

MASSAGE

When your hands with a delicacy all their own
Hovered over my skin, caressing the dark hair,
Yielding to the hardness of cartilage and bone

I remembered my father in his brief old age,
Sour with self-loathing, hawking into the stove
The soft black mucus. In the incomprehensible cage

Of his marriage, a wounded animal, love's pariah,
Padding the hard floor, sniffing the medical air,
Alone and fearing the beginning of nowhere.

And I wept for the touch he had never known,
The hand easing the skin, soothing the terminal bone:
The panther, uncaged, in its darkness coming home.

SPRIGS OF ROSEMARY

I bring this sprig of rosemary; but what is rosemary for?
It is for releasing memory, for increasing memory's store.

Yet few memories come back; childhood oppresses
With its weight of sullen fears. My life regresses

Into the black. I cannot remember what I said or did.
A haphazard crow flies at an angle to the wood.

So many memories gone into the gap under the falling wave,
Ash to the metallic fire, the blankness of the grave.

There's a paradox here. I pluck rosemary to mark what's absent,
To acknowledge what is over with aromatic scent,

To let it go with grace - and then I remember images of you:
The lapis lazuli against the whiteness of your neck, your sigh

At the eternal candour of its blue.You are the one somewhere
In my imagination with sprigs of rosemary in her hair

And sprays of bay leaves in her hands, whose radiant eyes
Bring back, at memory's furthest root, the glint of Paradise.

THE DANCE OF SYLLABLES

Come now my holy lyre
Find your voice and speak to me

Sappho

A WHITE DARK-SCENTED ROSE

Love, listen to these words that run obliquely,
That never quite declare their aim, nor yield
What they appear to promise. Strange. Haunted.

Labile. Remember, last night, how the dark wind
Blew the transfiguring snow across the Downs
Over the familiar dusty paths? Like that, but not

Like that at all. Or imagine a white dark-scented rose
In some unknown garden, petal by petal, silently
Opening, silently closing, and no God watching.

Like that, but not like that at all. These words
Rise on their cadence. They cast a further spell
Until we enter an estrangement which feels like home.

MOMENTS OF BEING

There are no axioms to silence critics –
There are only moments and metaphors
Which make the blood course faster for their stimulus.

They explode into imagination with such force
They create a firmament, a site for angels.
In our galactic skulls live all the gods.

And there's always the gift of language. Sudden speech.
Words which break the sullen water to cut
A silver track of dripping light

Or lift like calligraphic swifts into a holocaust sky
To scrawl their zig-zag stanzas –
As the moon rises and drifts. Silent.

Eucharistic.
White.

THEN LOVE ME FOR MY FLYING

Remember Leonardo da Vinci? How as a young boy
He ran through the square unlocking cages
And shouting to the captive birds: *Fly now! Fly now!*
Love, never keep me caged beyond my will

For part of me is like a bird. An albatross –
Born of crag and wilderness - it rises motionless
Above the zig-zag traffic of the tides.
At night it glides across the pack-ice edges

Of the southern hemisphere, wings stretched
Between polluted water and TV satellites.
The zero winds burn clean the toxic air.
This is a shaman's world, a pristine life.

Then love me for my flying - my oceanic eyes –
The whiteness of my neck - my sea-bird cries.

THE SONG OF WORDS

Water cleans itself until each amber stone
Shines beneath the turbulence: clear, angular,
Eloquent. Even ancient rock and slate and bone

Now yield their natural reticence to chant
The power of water, to sing its lilting essence:
Sa la sa la liea siea - all the way to the distant

Estuary, the jade cormorant, gull's clamour.
We utter more than we can ever know –
For words like water crave the sea, flow under

Our intimate breath, slip under the ticking clock,
Sing in the eyes of the skull, rill in the jaws
Of death - the white spume gashing the rock:

Sa la sa la sa la
Liea siea

NEW POEMS

2001

OWL OF MINERVA

Turning off the main road into a side lane,
On a track with no name,
With no moon, with no stars, in the extreme

Darkness of a Norfolk night, with no maps,
No compass, no defences,
In the black-out of our blitzed senses,

We suddenly catch in the car's headlight,
Cutting through eyeless night,
Athene's bird: white benediction, radiant flight.

IN EXILE

(After Ovid and Mandelstam)

Indeploratum barbara terra teget
Unmourned, a barbarian earth shall cover me

Ovid in *Tristia*

The bronzed horses drop their heads to graze - the bracken rusts
Like the imperium of Rome. Time's provincial drizzle erases
A classical spring's gold. I walk the Autumn woods -

A shadow in the cold. This is a flat barbaric place to compose
A thousand formal elegies. And now I detect the lie in Caesar's pose:
His effeminate cheeks, that murderous hook-nose.

How soon the glitter of rhetoric corrodes. Without a Corinthian
ideal -
A fluted column, a dancing frieze - life slows, becomes mechanical
And mean. In this brawling ghetto I watch an imperial

Civilization judder and go down. The locals murder for a fleece,
Kill their time, mouth a garbled Greek. Oh, may this iron state
Slide under the waters of its fraudulence without a trace

And may our corroded language receive the cleansing oil of grace.
I shall die an outcast here but will come back in children's games:
A clear eye. A fearless foot. A rising cadence.

THE STORM CLOUD

John Ruskin describes the weather near the end of the 19th Century

A thousand miles square and five miles down
It blows in, blots out the sun.
I call it the plague- wind; I name it the storm-cloud.

What does it feel like? A terminus. The stop of time.
The strawberries rot on their stems –
For a month or more now not an hour of sunshine -

And the roses in the garden hang sponges of vinegar.
I'm a hunter of hieroglyphs;
In every metallic drop of rain I see a barren star.

And on stormy days leaves against the open window
Tremble continuously and hiss into
Sulphur-mists. Aspens of the apocalypse! Winds blow

The belching smoke across the stricken land. I read
The age in smouldering rivulets of
Fire, black snow, low toxic clouds, lists of children dead

Or slowly dying. Tonight I see a burning child
Rise through the millennial flames,
A charred Christ who sings: *we're at the thresh-hold* –

The uncreation now begins. Half-mad, I record what I can -
Cracked conduit of visions
And blizzards: *oh blanched sun, oh withered grass, oh blinded man.*

BARN OWL

Almost a revelation this morning - the barn owl in the shopping mall,
Perching on a gloved hand, clawing the simulated leather.
I was drawn at once to its primitive power, its sheer presence.
Its fine wings quivered and shuddered in the fluorescent glare

Of the cramped precinct. I fell for the fall of its white feathers –
The wings like priest's vestments tapering into yellow and orange.
Its eyes hypnotized mine with their circles of primeval darkness.
I imagined the bird navigating the wildest night, its beak open,

Its claws fast, a daemon of terror, or wavering on rounded wings
In the dazzling trauma of some car's lights. Then I remembered
Another owl. It stood paralysed on a painted bough, lifeless
In the glass dome of my childhood. A hesitant boy I longed

To smash the polished glass, take the victim in my hands
And ease it through the windows into a healing sky –
And now that owl was fluttering before my open eyes,
Splaying its shamanic wings, emitting its long-caged cries.

ROAD-SIDE DEATHS

On the same day two animals on the track to the coast –

First, a red fox slumped by the steep lane's bank.
It lay with its front paws delicately crossed as if asleep
But its jaws were clenched in a snarl and its entrails stank

On the hot tarmac. I yanked it by its back leg and dropped
It into the cool shadow and scrub on the unseen slope,
Plucking what sparse leaves I could to green its matted head.

On the next stretch a badger sprawled near the road's ditch
In a swirl of metal heat and carbon monoxide.
I imagined the driver - the musak drumming at fever pitch -

Slamming the beast and speeding on. In his small inferno
What did he see but a TV blur on the car's dark screen?
What did he hear but the crass murderous crescendo

Of the disco beat? I picked up the unmourned carcass
And tossed it on the scorched grass. There are no elegies.
No rites. No burials. The glinting cars swish past.

THE SWAN

I had read of swans, of course, and could recite their names:
The Mute, the Bewick and the Whooper. I knew their habitats:
Inland reservoirs, pastoral meadows, meandering rivers,

Suburban shallows. That they were protected by provenance
And law I also knew but I disliked their frigid elegance,
Their studied gliding movements, their balletic stance.

The calm display of their choreography invited metaphors
Of status without power, taste without prophecy: icons
For heraldic shields, emblems for mugs, scenes for jigsaws -

And then I saw the swan above the river's tidal water,
A prodigy of driven white, its huge wings whirring over
My astounded head, its webbed feet dripping silver

In the mist and light. No beginning. No middle. No end...
Not a word on my tongue... *Mysterium Tremendum*.

RED FOX

What were we looking for? Each morning as the train raced
Between urban stations - disused, vandalized - we watched
The fields glide by. Patches of chemical green, withered marsh,

Scarred land. From the window we scanned the margins,
Impatient to claim whatever stricken life ran at the edges –
To catch the red fox sprinting reckless under spiked iron ledges,

Its tail scorching tinder ground. And momentarily we caught him –
In his new habitat, loping by a scree of cars, a metal mound,
A smouldering stream - or suspended between action, his green

Eyes staring, his paws reading the raw brail of the broken earth.
Gone almost before seen - like a sudden image come to birth
In a deep-sleep dream...*Fox! Fox!* we shouted - only to witness

The trauma of his absence. But his rank beauty entered us,
Taunted our tamed hours, haunted us like a god - lost
In that corroded hinterland. Yet radiant still. *Deus absconditus.*

ASPEN LEAVES

As I drift down, almost asleep, I am at the Oak Woods
Pushing the chipped blue door until it opens
Into the walled garden. Box-hedge greens the cinder paths;

They go to the deep pond. In the silver sheen small fish
Rise and fall, the shadows of aspen leaves. I hear the bees
Buzz against the dusty slate, taste the ripe peach's

Sweet pulp on my tongue, see the line of green beech
Opening into the fields, the gleam of the furrowed sea,
That far horizon. In a single instant - all within my reach.

But then the summer light fades fast and grandfather
Sits silent in his chair and the fire is all but out and there's
A handkerchief over his eyes and his book has fallen to the floor

And I'm running up the stairs and there's no light from the moon
And there's a wind gusting under the eaves
And then a hush and - only leaves and leaves and leaves

DRIFTING SNOW

I wake in the dead hours, restive, pulled from sleep.
The bitter air weighs lighter. Out on the urban street
The all-night traffic's hum is muffled, distant,

Dream-like.Under the high hooded metal light
A flurry of snow fills the phosphorescent night.
The neighbours' parked cars are shrouded white.

And in the hush of silence I pray for the wind to rise,
To drive the snow across the stricken land, to erase
This iron labyrinth, this concrete corrugated maze –

But then I'm trudging through the drifts, a child again
And there's not a familiar place I can recognize or name
And all my anxious footprints are quickly filling in

And the wind against my head is a spectral blade of ice
And the heavy leaden sky is running out of light -
And there's nothing's here - but white on white on white

BLOWING DANDELION CLOCKS AT SEAFORD HEAD

As fledgling gulls glide over us
We leave the cliff's worn paths
For untrod grass, vetch, pink scabius,

Clover, dandelions - seeding late.
Casually we blow their frail freight
Over the cliff's ledge. Almost as delicate

As the air they ride, the seeds take flight -
Frail diaspora, an unlikely exodus –
Into the thunderous crashings of the tide.

How carelessly nature takes her chance
At the last moment, last gasp –
And we are part of that haphazard dance,

Walking together between seasons at
The high white edge, precarious too,
Blindly puffing ephemeral seeds, black

Specks of hope into the amorphous blue.
The sun sweats in the palm of our hands
Yet the breeze burns cool. *And can you*

Feel the winter coming in? I ask,
Wrapping my white silk scarf
Around your neck. Exquisitely you adjust

The gift until it warms your naked skin.
You do not speak but stand suspended,
Floating, as we sense the future sweeping in,

A dance, at least, for us. We pluck and free
Another rounded globe of seeds and watch
Them fly. A random light is blazing on the sea.

WIND CHIMES

Do you remember how we bought the wind chimes by chance
In that store on the industrial estate? Holding them in our hands
They resembled silver flutes, the small censored pipes of Pan;
They were full of the prospect of music, the magic of gamelan -

And we bought them at once. We tied them to a tree in the yard
And were enchanted for weeks as their bright silver sound
Rang through the rooms of our house - and then we no longer
Heard them. Perhaps they had become all too familiar?

Or had sultry weather come in and stifled the delicate chimes?
Whatever the reason - so busy our lives we seemed not to care.
Then last night I woke in the early hours. A wind was shaking
The house and in the jagged gaps of the storm I could hear

Magic of gamelan - the fragile chimes - and I knew they were ours,
Throwing their trembling silver out to the entropic stars.

ARS POETICA

It will listen to the arias of whales.
It will wake to the dawn yelp of the gull.
It will affirm the blue canticle of the skylark, the black
croak of the frog.
It will be schooled by the sibilance of water, be attuned
to the hard consonance of rock.
It will gut dictionaries.
It will eat etymologies.
It will eavesdrop on the spontaneous ramblings of children.
It will tour fairgrounds with a microphone.
It will tremble before the glance of Beauty.
It will taste the the white vinegar of death.
It will honour silence.
It will be a crucible open to stars and dust.
It will expound the laws of Quantum Mechanics and recite
the Proverbs of Blake.
It will aspire to the levity of the butterfly crossing nuclear zones.
It will be born in blood, rise in estrangement, climax in breath.
It will remain in quest.